CULTURES OF THE WORLD

ESTONIA

Michael Spilling

MARSHALL CAVENDISH
New York • London • Sydney

Reference edition published 1999 by
Marshall Cavendish Corporation
99 White Plains Road
Tarrytown
New York 10591

© Times Editions Pte Ltd 1999

Originated and designed by
Times Books International, an imprint of
Times Editions Pte Ltd

Printed in Malaysia

Library of Congress Cataloging-in-Publication Data:

Spilling, Michael.
    Estonia / Michael Spilling.
       p. cm.—(Cultures of the World)
    Includes bibliographical references and index.
    Summary: Introduces the geography, history, government,
economy, culture, and people of Estonia, the most northerly
and least populated of the three Baltic states.
    ISBN 0-7614-0951-3 (library binding)
    1. Estonia—Juvenile literature. [1. Estonia.] I. Title.
II. Series.
DK503.23.S65   1999
947.98—dc21   98–43682
                 CIP
                 AC

INTRODUCTION

A SMALL LAND OF FORESTS, lakes, and islands washed by the eastern shores of the Baltic Sea, the Republic of Estonia is a newly independent republic little known to the rest of the world. For five decades Estonia remained an unwilling part of the Soviet Union. For much of its history, this most northerly Baltic state has endured occupation by Russians, Germans, and Swedes.

Since gaining independence in 1991, Estonians have rediscovered their history, culture, and language, and are proud of their country's thriving economy and cultural renaissance. In recovering their nationhood and freedom and controlling their own destiny, Estonians have forged a newfound confidence and an increased national pride. Today the people of Estonia are laying the foundations for an economically vibrant democracy, integration with Western Europe, and closer ties with their most culturally similar neighbors in Scandinavia.

CONTENTS

Homemade dolls in traditional national dress.

CONTENTS

An Estonian policeman.

GEOGRAPHY

SITUATED ON THE EASTERN SHORE of the Baltic Sea, the Republic of Estonia—or *Eesti Vabariik,* as it is called in Estonian—is the most northerly and least populated of the three Baltic states. This small, newly independent country is 17,457 square miles (45,226 square km) in area—slightly larger than Switzerland. Estonia's long coastline is washed by the Baltic Sea on the west and the Gulf of Finland on the north. The Baltic state of Latvia is in the south, while the Narva River and Lake Peipus divide Estonia from its large and powerful Russian neighbor in the east. Including the islands, Estonia has 2,360 miles (3,800 km) of highly indented coastline, very long for such a tiny country. Although geographically part of Eastern Europe, Estonia—unlike its Baltic neighbors Latvia and Lithuania—is more Nordic in character, a Scandinavian land stranded on the wrong side of the Baltic Sea. Tallinn, Estonia's capital, is just a 52-mile (84-km) boat ride from Helsinki, the capital of Finland.

Opposite and left: **Estonia is famous for its large deposits of limestone. Houses, farms, castles, churches, and countless stone walls have been constructed using this valuable grey stone.**

THE LAND

Estonia can be divided into two distinct geographic areas: a coastal region in the north and west that is characterized by low-lying marshes, lakes, and islands, and a plain in the east and south, which is higher in elevation, typically 160 feet (49 m) above sea level.

Only 10% of the land area is over 300 feet (91 m) high. Suur Munamägi ("Large Egg Hill") is Estonia's highest point at 1,040 feet (317 m).

The plain in the south is situated on the northern edge of the North European Plain— a vast, flat landscape that stretches westward from northern Germany, through Poland, the Baltic countries, and northern Russia. The higher part of the plain runs north to south through the eastern part of Estonia and includes the Pandivere plateau, the Otepää plateau, and the Haanji plateau. Southern and eastern Estonia is predominantly rural in character.

The low-lying areas in the west and north include the whole coastal area and have extensive marshlands, over 1,400 lakes, and some 1,500 islands. The northern coast, around the cities of Tallinn, Kohtla-Järve, and Narva, is home to much of Estonia's industry.

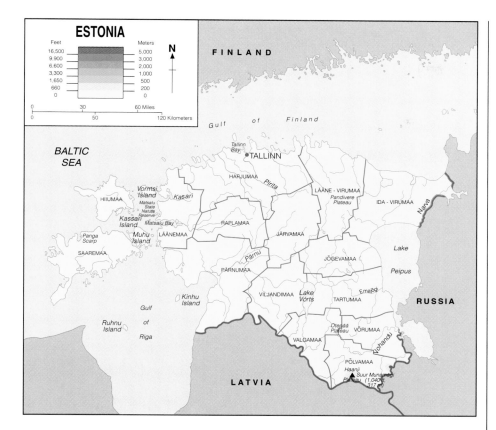

REGIONS

Estonia is divided into 15 *maakond* ("MAH-kont") or counties. In the north, Harjumaa is the country's most populous *maakond* and includes the capital, Tallinn. In the northeast are the two counties of Lääne-Virumaa and Ida-Virumaa. The three counties of Järvamaa, Jõgevamaa, and Viljandimaa occupy the center of Estonia. In the south, the *maakond* of Tartumaa includes the ancient city of Tartu. The other three counties in the south are Põlvamaa, Võrumaa, and Valgamaa. In the west, the *maakond* of Pärnumaa includes the historic city of the same name. Läänemaa covers the northwest coastal area of Estonia. The county of Raplamaa includes the administrative town of the same name. The island of Saaremaa is a separate *maakond*, which also includes the island of Muhu, as well as 500 smaller islands. The island of Hiiumaa is also a *maakond*.

Opposite: **Windmills still dot the countryside, reminders of the hundreds that were once used to power Estonia.**

9

CLIMATE AND SEASONS

Estonia has a temperate and sometimes humid climate. Winters are milder than in corresponding latitudes because cold air masses are warmed by passage over the Gulf Stream and the Baltic Sea. Consequently, warm air hits Estonia in the winter and cool air in the summer. Generally, the northern and western coastal areas have a milder climate than the higher, inland region. The inland areas in the south and east experience a more extreme continental climate, with hot summers and cold winters.

Winter arrives in November and does not end until March, or sometimes April. Spring and fall are generally cold and wet.

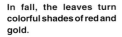

In fall, the leaves turn colorful shades of red and gold.

ISLAND RETREATS

Estonia's islands, which number over 1,500 and constitute as much as 10% of Estonia's total territory, contain perhaps the most unspoiled and secluded landscapes in the country. Only two islands are of any significant size: Saaremaa (1,030 square miles/2,670 square km) and Hiiumaa (382 square miles/990 square km). Saaremaa has a population of 40,000, while Hiiumaa is inhabited by 12,000 people. Clustered off the western shore of the mainland, the
islands have maintained a traditional, quiet, and distinctly Estonian way of life. The Soviet authorities helped maintain the islands' natural state. The islands were thought to be escape routes to the West because of their seclusion, so while some parts of Estonia were polluted by Soviet industrial projects, the islands were not developed. Military personnel were the only visitors to the islands for many years.

Saaremaa is a scenic island with many charming fishing villages, neat cottages, nature reserves, beach resorts, windmills, and pine forests. On the northern edge of the island there are some picturesque limestone formations. From here, the Panga Scarp, the island's highest cliff at 73 feet (22 m), offers a superb view of the clear, green Baltic Sea. The island includes a strange and unique phenomenon: the massive Kali crater, formed by a 1,000-ton (907-tonne) meteorite in the 8th century B.C. It is one of the most accessible meteorite craters in the world. Filled with opaque green water, some people think it looks like a large bowl of pea soup! The capital of Saaremaa, Kuressaare (population 17,000), has a well-preserved 14th century castle. To reach Saaremaa from the mainland, it is necessary to take a ferry to the smaller, neighboring island of Muhu. The causeway that links Muhu and Saaremaa is one of the most beautiful spots in Estonia, with the water colored green with swaying reeds. In the spring thousands of swans go there to mate. Muhu is Estonia's third largest island and has a population of 2,500.

Hiiumaa includes numerous stately homes and some remarkable lighthouses. The Kopu lighthouse was first lit in 1531 and is thought to be the third oldest, continuously operating lighthouse in the world. The capital of Hiiumaa, Kärdla, is a small town of some 4,000 people. Very few people live in the heart of the island, where there are peat bogs and swamps. Hiiumaa is rich in flora, and boasts over 900 species of plants, including rare orchids. Many of Estonia's artists have summer houses on Hiiumaa. The most popular spot for summer cottages, however, is Kassari, the largest of 400 islands that closely hug the southern coast of Hiiumaa. Junipers are Kassari's most common plant. They are used in every way imaginable: the wood for butter knives to stop the butter turning rancid; the branches for sauna switches; and the berries as a vodka spice.

LAKES AND RIVERS

Lakes are one of the country's most characteristic features. Lake Peipus, with an area of 1,350 square miles (3,500 square km), is the fourth largest lake in Europe and is considered one of the best fishing spots (it contains over 30 species of fish). Today it provides Estonia with 90% of its inland fishing production. Estonia's second largest lake, Võrts (104 square miles, 269 square km), is just west of the Otepää plateau. The lake is used mainly for fishing and as a reservoir.

Numerous rivers flow across Estonia's sandstone and limestone plains. The Väike-Emajõgi River springs from the Otepää highlands and flows into Lake Võrts; it emerges as the Emajõgi (meaning "mother river") to the north and winds its way eastward through Tartumaa, eventually flowing into Lake Peipus. At 130 miles (209 km), it is Estonia's longest river. The Pärnu River is 89 miles (143 km) long, while to the north, the Narva River (49 miles/79 km) links Lake Peipus to the Gulf of Finland. Other major rivers include the Põltsamaa, Vohandu, Kasari, and Pirita.

FLORA AND FAUNA

There are about 18,000 different species of wildlife in Estonia, of which more than half are insects, and 90 species of trees and shrubs. The most common tree is pine, followed by birch, aspen, and fir. Less numerous, though still common trees, include oak, alder, and spruce.

About 60 species of mammals live in Estonia, mainly woodland and forest creatures. The magnificent elk and other deer, wild boar, badgers, foxes, squirrels, and beavers are common inhabitants, while the rarer brown bears, wolves, and lynx can still be seen.

Estonia is also home to over 300 species of birds, including migrating geese, swans, ducks, and storks. Sixty species of birds are year-round residents, the most common of which are sparrows, blackbirds, woodcocks, and golden eagles. Estonia's national bird is the graceful barn swallow.

Above: **Cornflowers grow wild in the woodlands of Estonia.**

Left: **Lynx grow thick coats during the winter, sometimes up to 4 inches (10 cm) long. The fur is sought for trimming coats and hats.**

13

NATURE RESERVES

Although there are a number of nature reserves in Estonia, Lahemaa National Park is the country's only official national park. Established in 1971, it covers an area of 432 square miles (1,120 square km) on the northern coast. The park includes offshore islands and waters, coastal peninsulas and bays, beaches, forests, and peat bogs, as well as 14 lakes, eight rivers, and numerous waterfalls. It is home to elk, brown bear, lynx, cranes, mink, and migrating black storks. The park also contains a wealth of the huge boulders that dot the landscape of northern Estonia. The tallest of these is Tammispea, a massive 26 feet (8 m) high.

The Matsalu State Nature Reserve lies in Matsalu Bay on Estonia's western coast, south of Haapsalu. It is noted mainly for its bird habitats, including reed-beds, water-meadows, and coastal pastures. Species such as the avocet, sandwich tern, mute swan, and greylag goose can be found here. The reserve was established in 1957.

There are also nature reserves in the Otepää and Haanji highlands. The Haanji plateau is covered with wetlands and bogs, and is home to many migratory birds, such as storks. The Otepää highlands have a varied landscape that includes lakes, rivers, and forests.

Opposite: **A view from Toompea Hill above Tallinn.**

CITIES

As a predominantly rural country, Estonia has no cities of any great size. Nevertheless, the capital, Tallinn (population 440,000), is one of the most beautiful and picturesque cities in the Baltic region. Its streets seem to tumble down the side of a fortress-topped hill, Toompea, and spread out into Tallinn Bay. Originally established by Danish conquerors in the 13th century, Tallinn (meaning "Danish fortress") still has a strongly medieval character with cobbled sidewalks, walls, and numerous towers, turrets, and spires.

Tallinn has always been strategically important in the eastern Baltic and consequently has been occupied by Denmark, Sweden, and Russia in the course of its history. This has given the city a special, cosmopolitan atmosphere. The dominant influence is German, however, and much of the city has a strong medieval German flavor.

Many of the Hanseatic towers that were a part of the city's fortifications have been preserved, Pik Herman ("Fat Herman") being one of the most notable. Toompea—the name of the fortress and old town on the crest of the hill—derives from the German word *domberg*, meaning "cathedral mountain."

Tartu retains a sleepy, relaxed quality, despite its size.

Estonia's second city, Tartu (population 110,000), is located in the southeast of the country on the Emajõgi River. Tartu was first built as a stronghold in the 11th century by the grand duke of Kiev. Much of the old town has been destroyed in wars throughout Estonia's turbulent history, and most buildings now date from the 18th century. A university was established in Tartu in 1632, and ever since, the city has been considered the spiritual and cultural center of Estonia. Tartu was the center of the nationalist and cultural revival in the 19th century.

Located in the industrial northeast of Estonia on the Russian border, Narva (population 77,000) is Estonia's third largest city. It is separated from the Russian city of Ivangorod by the Narva River and is almost entirely populated by ethnic Russians. Narva is closer to Russia's traditional northern capital, St. Petersburg, than it is to Tallinn. Narva's heavy industries are a stark contrast to Estonia's predominantly rural character. The name "Narva" comes from the Baltic-Finnish word *narvaine*, meaning "the threshold." Narva was a German trading town as far back as the 12th century. The city was almost completely destroyed in World War II, and little of the historic town remains.

Kohtla-Järve (population 70,000), Estonia's fourth largest city, is 30 miles (48 km) west of Narva. It is a modern industrial city built 60 years ago as a result of oil-shale mining in the area. Pärnu (population 53,000) is Estonia's fifth largest city and is located on the Gulf of Riga. The town developed around a German fort built in the 13th century. It is Estonia's leading seaside resort and health spa.

THE AFFLICTED ENVIRONMENT

Throughout the Baltic states, environmental pollution has become a serious problem over the last few decades. Much of this damage is the result of poorly planned urban and industrial expansion under the Soviet regime. Water quality in Riga, the capital of Latvia, is so bad that in 1989 there was an outbreak of hepatitis A; Latvians have boiled all water since that time. The Baltic Sea has been the dumping ground for industrial waste for decades.

Pärnu, Haapsalu, Tallinn, Kohtla-Järve, and Narva—Estonia's main industrial centers—are all on or near the coast. The shallow Baltic Sea is currently so polluted that Estonian fishing vessels are forced to travel to all parts of the globe to stay in business. Over-fishing in the Soviet period has also resulted in drastically depleted fish-stocks. Estonia is working hard to meet all the European Union (EU) environmental requirements in order to obtain membership in the EU. A clean-up strategy has been instigated that will run until 2010, including upgrades to the water and sewage systems.

Much of the pollution has been caused by Estonia's attempt to solve its energy shortages. The oil-shale mines around Kohtla-Järve have created great slag heaps. These mountains of waste contain toxic metals and organic compounds that are washed by the rain into the sea. When the oil-shale is burned it produces a residue of petrified ash that has ruined the countryside in the northeast of Estonia. Twenty million tons (18 million tonnes) of oil-shale is burned in thermal power plants at Narva each year, emitting 380,000 tons (344,660 tonnes) of sulphur dioxide. This gas not only pollutes the air in the northeast, but is carried across the Gulf of Finland by the wind, where it pollutes Finland's forests. Unfortunately, the oil-shale mines produce 50% of Estonia's thermal output, and so production continues.

On the positive side, in rural areas Soviet mismanagement and neglect has led to a proliferation of wildlife. Inefficient agricultural management caused an increase in forests, providing habitats for local wildlife. In addition, many coastal areas were out-of-bounds for military reasons, so many beautiful beaches remained unspoiled for 50 years. Wildlife habitats that have disappeared in the rest of Europe still exist in Estonia.

GUSTAVUS II ADOLPHUS

REX SUECIAE

HISTORY

ESTONIANS HAVE EXISTED as a clearly identifiable people since ancient times. Despite this long-acknowledged identity, they have rarely been masters of their own domain. As one of the smallest and least populated countries in Europe, Estonia's history has been one of domination by outsiders—Sweden, Denmark, Poland, Russia, and, most significantly, Germany have all left strong impressions.

Estonia enjoyed its first, short-lived period of independence from 1918 to 1940. Those years of independence were a source of inspiration to future generations of Estonians and provided them with the motivation to grasp their freedom when the Soviet empire crumbled in the late 1980s.

BEGINNINGS

Estonians were first described at length by the Roman historian Tacitus in *Germania*: "The Fenni [Estonians] are astonishingly savage and disgustingly poor. They have no proper weapons, no horses, no homes. They eat wild herbs, dress in skins, and sleep on the ground ... Unafraid of anything that man or God can do to them, they have reached a state that few human beings can attain: for these men are so well content that they do not even need to pray for anything."

In the 5th century Slavic tribes appeared south of present-day Estonia. Estonians built fortified villages to defend themselves, but without a king or nobility around which to form a central power base, they were quickly defeated.

In the 9th century, Estonia was a part of the Viking trade route from Scandinavia to the Slavic countries, Byzantium, and the Caspian Sea. Around this time, agricultural improvements were made: households owned cultivated land, while land and forest surrounding a village was commonly shared by the villagers.

Throughout the Soviet occupation of Estonia, the United States government never recognized the legitimacy of Soviet rule and continued to deal with the Estonian Consulate in New York City as the legal representative of Estonia.

Opposite: **A statue of Gustavus Adolphus, king of the Swedish empire that included Estonia in the 16th and 17th centuries.**

CRUSADER CONQUEST

In the 11th and 12th centuries, the Slavs made many incursions into Estonia but failed to establish supremacy. The Danes and Swedes also made unsuccessful attempts to Christianize the Estonians. German monks began preaching Christianity along the Baltic coast in 1180, but with little success.

In 1193 the Pope in Rome declared a Baltic Crusade in an attempt to convert the Baltic people to Christianity. German merchants were eager to open up the Baltic region to German trade and supported the Pope's proclamation. Under the leadership of Albert von Buxhoevden, German knights responded to the Pope's call by forming the Knights of the Sword and mounting a military invasion of the Baltic coast in 1200. They wore the famous crusader capes with a red cross on a white background. The

A sketch of a battle fought by the German knights.

knights soon established the city of Riga in 1201. By 1208 they had subdued the Livs and Latgalians, tribes to the south of Estonia, and occupied most of present-day Lithuania and Latvia.

From 1208 onward, the German knights turned their attention to Estonia. The Estonians lost men steadily, while the knights constantly replenished their forces with fresh crusaders from Germany. The Estonian military leader, Lembitu, organized a fierce resistance, but he was killed in 1217. Estonia's lack of a centralized command or power structure made it difficult for them to unite and resist invasion. Tribes and clans were conquered in turn and forcibly baptized by the fierce crusaders. Most of southern Estonia was subdued by 1218. Northern Estonia was not conquered until 1219, when Albert's ally, the crusading King Valdemar II of Denmark, captured the site of Tallinn and founded the city. By 1220 all of Estonia was under German and Danish control except the island of Saaremaa. The island was finally subdued by the knights in the winter of 1227 when the Baltic froze and they were able to mount an assault with ease.

GERMAN RULE

In 1237 the Knights of the Sword joined the much stronger German-based Teutonic Order, one of the largest and most powerful crusading organizations in Europe. The crusaders' attempt to expand north was brought to an end by the Russians in 1242 at the famous Battle of the Ice on Lake Peipus when the legendary Alexander Nevsky (1220–63) decisively

Alexander Nevsky, the legendary hero who defeated the Knights of the Sword.

Martin Luther, German Protestant reformer and founder of the Lutheran movement.

defeated the knights. The area known as Livonia came under the control of the Teutonic Order. Northern Estonia was ruled by the Danes.

The Teutonic Order absorbed Estonia into the Hanseatic League, a loose trading association of German towns and states along the Baltic coast. Estonia's primitive agrarian economy was soon transformed into one of the best farming and trading communities of the Middle Ages.

In 1343 the Estonian peasantry rose up against their foreign masters, determined to end their subjugation. Tallinn was besieged, and many Germans were killed on the islands of Saaremaa and Hiiumaa. Thousands of Estonians were slaughtered in revenge, and no further uprisings were attempted for 200 years. In 1346 Denmark, whose power had been waning, sold northern Estonia to the Livonian Order, a branch of the Teutonic Order.

The Germans dominated Baltic culture for the next two centuries. German merchants controlled commerce and the town councils, while German nobles owned most of the land. The Estonians and Latvians made up the peasant class—95% of the population.

END OF THE TEUTONIC ORDER

At the end of the 15th century, two new powers emerged around the borders of Livonia: Poland-Lithuania, a united kingdom to the south, and Muscovite Russia. Territorial disputes led to wars between Poland and the Teutonic Order in 1454 and 1519.

In 1519 the head of the Livonian Order, Grand Master Albert, met Martin Luther (1483–1546), the great Christian reformer. Luther advised Albert to secularize his vast estates and save paying any more taxes to Rome. In 1524 Tallinn's church synod adopted the principles of the Reformation, and the other towns in Estonia soon followed. Henceforth, Estonia became a Protestant country. The ordinary Estonians, however, remained largely indifferent to these changes, since the majority of the clergy were German.

The destruction of Rome's influence led to the break-up and eventual dissolution of the Teutonic and Livonian orders in 1561. The Livonian Wars plunged the country into 25 years of turmoil. The Russians, under Ivan the Terrible (1530–84), penetrated deep into Estonian territory in 1558, devastating the area and weakening the military power of the Livonian Order. In the 1560s Poland-Lithuania and Sweden fought for control of Estonia, and Russia reentered the fray in the 1570s.

In 1584 Sweden—having expelled the Russians—emerged as the dominant power in northern Estonia, while Poland maintained control of Livonia. In 1599 secessionist conflicts led to further wars between Sweden and Poland-Lithuania. Estonia was again ravaged by foreign armies, and the Estonian population suffered heavy casualties from war, disease, and famine. In 1629, at the Truce of Altmark, Poland-Lithuania surrendered the major part of Livonia to Sweden, leaving the Scandinavians the dominant power in the Baltic.

Ivan the Terrible, leader of the Russians.

SWEDISH INFLUENCE

Following the Truce of Altmark, the Swedish empire included much of the Baltic region, including Estonia, Livonia, Finland, Western Pomerania, and Bremen. Many of the German-descended Baltic barons were given land by the Swedish king Gustavus Adolphus (1594–1632) in an attempt to win their loyalty. Unfortunately, the German landlords abused their position by increasing taxes and extorting excessive unpaid labor from the peasants. Isolated rebellions broke out but were not successful.

THE GREAT NORTHERN WAR (1700–21)

In 1697 Charles XII (1682–1718, pictured left) was crowned king of Sweden. Russia, Denmark, and Poland judged that the time was ripe to end Swedish domination of the Baltic region and concluded an alliance in 1699. A titanic struggle ensued between Charles and Peter the Great of Russia. In November 1700, a Russian force of 35,000 men led by Peter marched on Narva, which was held by a small Swedish garrison. Charles hurried to the town's aid and plunged his newly arrived army of 8,000 men into battle. The poorly equipped and badly trained Russians were taken by surprise, and Peter lost every piece of artillery he possessed. However, instead of pursuing his advantage and pressing on to Moscow, Charles turned his attention to Poland.

With Charles's army in Poland, Peter reinvaded the Baltic region and captured Narva and Tartu in 1704. In 1708 every major building in Tartu was destroyed: according to an old saying, "No dog barked and no cock crowed from Tartu to Narva."

In 1708 Charles renewed his campaign against Russia through the Ukraine. However, at the Battle of Poltava (1709) Charles's army was totally destroyed by the Russians. Over the next 10 years Sweden's Baltic possessions were seized by Denmark, Prussia, and Russia. Having gained Finland in 1714, Peter launched an invasion of Sweden in 1719. At the Peace of Nystad in 1721, Sweden was forced to concede all the Baltic provinces to Russia, and Estonia came under Russian control.

The Swedish king Charles XI (1656–97) attempted to curb the power of the landlords. Baltic barons who could not prove land ownership by presenting title deeds were made tenants of the crown or replaced by Swedish landlords. Education was introduced at parish level, and in the 1630s the first books in Estonian appeared. Printing shops were opened in Tartu and Tallinn. In 1632 a university was established at Tartu, and by 1688 there were over 1,000 students in schools throughout Estonia and Livonia.

TSARIST RULE

Swedish influence ended in the eastern Baltic following the Great Northern War (1700–21). Peter I (1672–1725), called Peter the Great, finally realized his ambition of securing Russia's northern border and brought the Baltic permanently under Russian control. In 1703 Peter also built the city of St. Petersburg at the mouth of the Neva River, providing Russia with a permanent outlet to the Baltic Sea and a future northern capital.

Initially, Russian rule meant few changes for the Estonians. Like the Swedes before him, Peter sought to win over the German landlords by giving them more power. The landlords, who constituted only 1% of the population, controlled the administration, police, schools, and justice system, as well as owning all the land. In 1795 Tsar Alexander I (1777–1825) appointed a governor-general to administer the Baltic region. Diets (assemblies) were set up in Estonia, Livonia, and Saaremaa, and were run by 12 councillors who were elected for life.

Tsar Alexander II (seated) with his son (later Alexander III) and the Tsarina.

Tsar Alexander III in full uniform.

Writing in 1695, the chronicler Christian Kelch records: "Estonia is the landlord's heaven, the clergy's paradise, the stranger's gold mine, and the peasant's hell."

In 1739 the Rosen Declaration—written by Baron von Rosen, chairman of the Livonian diet—formalized the practices of centuries-old serfdom. Landlords were legally entitled to buy and sell peasants as they pleased, decide marriages, and administer corporal punishment. Peasants were also selected by lottery to serve as conscripts in the Russian army. During a visit to the Baltic provinces in 1764, Tsarina Catherine II (1729–96) was distressed at the appalling conditions of the serfs and recommended reforms. However, the German landlords ignored most of her suggestions. Peasant unrest in 1805, 1817, 1820, and 1858 had little effect.

Conditions did improve for the peasants following the abolition of serfdom in 1861 by Tsar Alexander II (1818–81). Peasants were allowed to pay money to rent their land, rather than paying rent in kind (usually labor), were free to conduct their own business, and could choose their own marriage partners without asking the landlord's permission. The barons were no longer allowed to buy and sell peasants or to use corporal punishment. Nevertheless, the best land remained in the possession of the landlords and peasants were still required to serve in the army and pay a heavy poll tax. Although they had gained their personal freedom, economic hardships continued to oppress the peasants.

In the 19th century, Estonia began to develop an industrial base, mainly factories manufacturing paper, glass, and textiles. The urban population rapidly increased, and by the 1860s Estonians were the majority in all urban centers for the first time. They were allowed to elect their own town assemblies and choose some town administrators.

Tsar Alexander III (1845–94) increased the Russification of the Baltic region and Russian administrators replaced the Baltic Germans in the judiciary and police force. Misdemeanors were harshly punished by the censorial Tsarist police.

CONSCRIPTION

In Tsarist Russia military conscription was dreaded by the peasants, who could be sent to the far-flung reaches of the Russian empire to fight wars and suffer hardship and disease. Lady Eastlake describes the situation in her travel memoirs, *A Residence on the Shores of the Baltic* (1841):

"From the moment that the peasant of the Baltic provinces draws the fatal lot no. 1, he knows that he is a Russian, and, worse than that, a Russian soldier, and not only himself, but every son from that hour born to him; like the executioner's office in Germany, a soldier's life is hereditary ... If wars and climate and sickness and hardship spare him, he returns after four-and-twenty years of service—his language scarce remembered, his religion changed, and with not a ruble in his pocket—to seek his daily bread by his own exertions for the remainder of his life, or to be chargeable to his parish, who by this time have forgotten that he ever existed, and certainly wish he had never returned."

Under Tsarist martial law, all political parties were dissolved, and radical Estonians were forced to flee abroad to escape capture.

NATIONAL AWAKENING

In the latter half of the 19th century, social reforms, the growth of manufacturing, and increased prosperity led to a growing sense of national consciousness among urban Estonians. Tartu University taught Estonian language and Estonian folklore, local newspapers were published, and a genuine Estonian intelligentsia developed. Radical, left-wing politics made an impact in Russia for much of the latter half of the 19th century.

In January 1905 widespread disillusionment with the regime in Russia ignited a country-wide revolution that immediately spread to Estonia. Workers went on strike in Tallinn, Pärnu, and Narva, and students protested in Tartu. German property became the target of arson attacks. Protests in Russia were suppressed by troops, and many thousands of people were killed.

At an All-Estonian Congress in Tartu in November 1905, both liberals and radicals demanded Estonian autonomy and a halt to Russification. The Tsarist authorities declared martial law to suppress the fledgling political movement, and workers scattered into the countryside and began looting and burning the country manors. As a consequence, troops were sent to Estonia and many revolutionaries were arrested and sentenced to death.

INDEPENDENCE WON

The outbreak of World War I in 1914 did not have much effect on Estonia. However, German war goals included occupying the eastern edge of the Baltic and turning it into an area for future German settlement. Many of the German barons in the Baltic secretly supported this aim and viewed with alarm the growing aspirations of the Baltic peoples. Most Estonians supported the Russian fight against the imperialistic Germans, and 100,000 Estonians were drafted into the Russian army.

In 1917 the debilitating effects of a disastrous war, food shortages, and weak government led to social unrest throughout Tsarist Russia. The Tsarist government quickly collapsed and a provisional government under the leadership of Alexander Kerensky came to power.

In Russia, workers' movements sprang up, and power was effectively split between government and workers.

On March 26, 1917, 40,000 workers demonstrated in downtown Tallinn. In response, the Kerensky government provisionally decreed home rule for Estonia. An Estonian National Council, called the *Maapäev*, was established, and a provisional government was set up with Konstantin Päts (1874–1956) as premier.

In November the Bolsheviks, under the leadership of Vladimir Lenin and Leon Trotsky, stormed the Winter Palace in St. Petersburg, igniting the first sparks of the Russian Revolution. In Tallinn the Bolsheviks also took control of the city and established a puppet government. However, within two months German forces had advanced as far as Tallinn, routing the communists. On February 24, 1918, the underground *Maapäev* declared Estonian independence. The next day German forces occupied the city, arrested many Estonian leaders, and claimed sovereignty over the Baltic states. Päts fled the country.

When war ended in November 1918, the retreating Germans left a gaping power vacuum. Päts and the independence movement again proclaimed Estonian independence, and the Bolshevik army promptly invaded Estonia. The Estonians received military assistance from Britain, Finland, Sweden, and Denmark; all supported Estonian calls for independence. The Estonian general Johannes Laidoner (1884–1953) led the Estonian army on a counteroffensive in January 1919. By the summer of 1919, the Estonians had been so successful that they had advanced to the edge of Riga in Latvia. Estonia had finally secured its borders.

Elections were held in April 1919 and Estonia's first Constituent Assembly was formed, with August Rei (1886–1963) as president. A coalition of socialists and liberals was represented in the assembly. A constitution was adopted in June 1920, and in 1921 Estonia gained international recognition and was admitted to the League of Nations. Estonia was an independent state for the first time in its history. In 1924 the communists attempted a coup in Tallinn but failed miserably. The Communist Party was thereafter outlawed in Estonia.

INDEPENDENCE LOST

In 1939 Soviet Russia and Nazi Germany signed the infamous Molotov-Ribbentrop agreement, a non-aggression pact that was to seal the fate of Estonia, Latvia, and Lithuania for the next 50 years—the Baltic states were to become Russian territories in exchange for Soviet non-interference when Germany invaded Poland.

Estonia was soon occupied by 100,000 Soviet troops. Thousands of Estonians were deported to the Union of Soviet Socialist Republics (USSR), including Päts and other political leaders. In August 1941 Estonia was officially incorporated into the USSR as a constituent republic, bringing an end to Estonia's short-lived independence.

Opposite: **World War II veterans gather each year to remember the war.**

Below: **Crowds gathered in Tallinn's Victory Square to support Estonia's incorporation into the Soviet Union.**

WORLD WAR II

In June 1941 Nazi Germany invaded Russia. By the end of August the Germans had swept through the Baltic states and captured the whole of mainland Estonia. By the end of the year they had advanced within a short distance of Moscow. The Germans were welcomed as liberators in Estonia, until it became obvious they were an occupation force. Estonians were deported to Germany as forced labor and a puppet administration was set up to rule the country. In 1942 the Germans recruited 500 Estonian volunteers to fight against the Russians in a special Estonian legion.

The Russians began a huge counteroffensive following their victory at the Battle of Stalingrad in 1942–43. By January 1944 the Soviet army had recaptured much of European Russia and had reached the Estonian border at Narva. Faced with the prospect of renewed Soviet occupation, the leader of the Estonian resistance, Jüri Üluots, called for Estonians to defend the city. For more than six months, 45,000 volunteers fought alongside the Germans in an attempt to stop the Soviet advance. However, by September 1944, the Red army had again conquered Estonia. Many Estonians fled west to Europe or to Finland to avoid living under Soviet rule.

SOVIET OPPRESSION

War casualties, deportations, and fleeing refugees reduced Estonia's population from a prewar level of 1.13 million to 850,000 by the end of the 1940s. A small anti-Russian resistance continued to fight from forest bases, but they were ineffective against the might of the Soviet army.

The 1950s were a difficult time for Estonians, and many people suffered under Soviet dictator Joseph Stalin's harsh regime: political opponents, intellectuals, and anyone believed to be a German collaborator were deported to Siberian labor camps. The Soviet administration also introduced a cultural Russification in a systematic attempt to eradicate Estonian national consciousness. Estonian history was rewritten, national monuments destroyed, and books suppressed.

Despite Soviet oppression, Estonian national consciousness remained strong. In the post-Stalin era, Estonians began to demonstrate for civil rights. Dissent reached its height in the Baltic states in 1979 on the 40th anniversary of the Molotov-Ribbentrop Pact.

INDEPENDENCE REGAINED

Soviet president Mikhail Gorbachev's policies of *glasnost* ("openness") and *perestroika* ("restructuring") led to a national renaissance in Estonia. Estonian cultural life flourished, a free press developed, political parties were formed, and religion was openly practiced again.

In August 1991 a failed military coup in Moscow by communist hard-liners effectively ousted Mikhail Gorbachev and led to an immediate break-up of the Soviet Union. Estonia declared full independence on August 20, 1991. It declined to join the successor to the USSR, the Commonwealth of Independent States (CIS), preferring to completely sever ties with Russia.

Mourners bring flowers to the spot where three people died resisting the coup.

GOVERNMENT

AS PART OF THE SOVIET UNION, Estonia was governed for 50 years as a province with little separate administrative bureaucracy or political autonomy. An Estonian parliament did exist—the Estonian Supreme Soviet—but as a local branch of the Communist Party it could only implement decisions made in Moscow.

Since independence, Estonia has had to build a new system of government, a task that the country has achieved with remarkable success in a short time. The Estonian government consists of an elected president, who is the head of state, and a single legislative assembly, the *Riigikogu* ("REE-ki-ko-ku"), led by the prime minister, who is the head of the government.

There have been frequent changes of prime minister and various realignments of government coalitions since independence. Between 1991 and 1997 there were three separate parliaments and seven changes of government. Despite this apparent political instability, government policy on political and economic reform has remained consistent, and reforms have continued at a rapid pace. The government has the confidence of the Estonian people and enjoys a great deal of popular support. Much of this support is a result of Estonia's highly successful transformation to a free-market economy. A new legal framework for business was quickly established, while a civil code for property, plus laws on competition, enterprise, and bankruptcy were also introduced.

The Estonian government is keen to avoid being tainted with accusations of corruption or unfair dealing, allegations often leveled at fledgling administrations in post-communist Eastern Europe. Any suspected offences are swiftly dealt with. For example, an Estonian ministry official was dismissed from his post for using his ministry cars to transport his wife and children on unofficial business.

Opposite: **Two soldiers walk past the Estonian Parliament in Tallinn.**

RESTORATION OF INDEPENDENCE

In 1988, the Estonian Supreme Soviet declared limited political sovereignty. A pro-reformist party, the Estonian Popular Front (EPF), gained seats in the Estonian Supreme Soviet in 1990. A parallel ruling body, the Congress of Estonia, was also formed by more radical parties demanding a restitution of the independent republic. Edgar Savisaar became the prime minister of the Supreme Soviet. Estonia's name, flag, and anthem were restored, although declared invalid by the Soviet leadership. A national referendum was held in March 1991, when 78% of Estonians (including many ethnic minorities) responded in favor of independence.

Estonia and many other Soviet republics declared independence in August, as soon as the coup in Moscow failed. This led to the immediate disintegration of the USSR.

POLITICS SINCE INDEPENDENCE

As a result of the deteriorating economic situation, Edgar Savisaar resigned as prime minister in January 1992. He was replaced by Tiit Vähi, who formed a transitional government. A Constitutional Assembly was formed, including delegates from both the Supreme Council and Congress of Estonia. A new constitution was adopted following a referendum, which provided for a 101-seat parliament, the *Riigikogu,* and a presidency with limited powers. Estonia's first free parliamentary elections were held in September, with 38 parties participating. The Fatherland alliance won 29 seats, making it the largest party in the *Riigikogu*. The Secure Home alliance, made up of many former communists, gained 17 seats, while the EPF-led Popular Front alliance won 15 seats. The Fatherland alliance soon formed a coalition with the Estonian National Independence Party. The leader of the Fatherland alliance, Mart Laar, became prime minister.

Mart Laar, former Estonian prime minister.

The new center-right government possessed few links with the old Soviet establishment. Several ministers were less than 35 years old, while many others were recently returned émigrés. Following a series of scandals and political defections, Laar was forced to resign as prime minister in 1994. He was replaced by Andres Tarand, leader of the Moderates.

Estonia's second post-independence parliamentary elections, held in 1995, was contested by 30 parties. Forty-one seats were won by an alliance of the Estonian Coalition Party and the Rural Union. A coalition of the newly established Estonian Reform Party won 19 seats and the Estonian Center Party gained 16 seats. For the first time, the Russian minority were

Lennart Meri was re-elected for a second term as president in 1996.

represented in the *Riigikogu* by the Our Home is Estonia alliance, which won six seats. The successors to the Communist Party failed to win any seats. Supported by the Estonian Center Party, Vähi, leader of the Estonian Coalition Party, became prime minister once again. Savisaar, the leader of the Estonian Center Party, became deputy prime minister. However, Savisaar was forced to resign later in 1995 when it was discovered he had been secretly recording conversations with other politicians. A new coalition was formed with the Reform Party, and Vähi continued as prime minister.

Vähi resigned as prime minister in February 1997 following allegations of corrupt real estate dealings in Tallinn. The deputy chairman of the Estonian Coalition Party, Mart Siimann, a former journalist, was nominated the new prime minister.

PRESIDENTIAL ELECTIONS

Estonia's first presidential elections, held in fall 1992, were inconclusive; no candidate won a majority, but four main candidates emerged. Following a second round of voting, Lennart Meri was declared the winner. Meri is a highly cultured man, the son of an Estonian dissident who was deported to Siberia by the Soviet authorities. A student of Estonian history, he has written travel accounts and a number of books on Estonian cultural identity and history, and made movies about the development of the Finno-Ugric peoples. He is also fluent in many major European languages and has translated works from French, English, and Russian into Estonian. Meri was elected president a second time in 1996.

THE RIIGIKOGU

Legislative power rests with Estonia's state assembly, the *Riigikogu*. The *Riigikogu*'s 101 members are elected for a term of four years by a system of proportional representation. They must be 21 years or older. Estonian citizens over the age of 18 can vote in national elections and referendums. The *Riigikogu* adopts laws, decides on the holding of referendums, elects the president of the republic, and ratifies the national budget. The *Riigikogu* also elects from its members a chairman who directs the work and procedures of the assembly.

Executive power is held by the Council of Ministers, or government, which is formed from members of the *Riigikogu*. The Council of Ministers consists of the prime minister, who is the head of the government, and other ministers. The prime minister has the task of forming the Council of Ministers, whose members are usually selected from the leading political parties. The Council of Ministers implements policy decisions and legislation, coordinates the work of government institutions, submits draft legislation to the *Riigikogu*, and organizes relations with foreign states.

The president of the republic is the head of state. The president is elected for a term of five years by a secret ballot in the *Riigikogu* and must gain a two-thirds majority. President Lennart Meri has held the post since 1992. Presidential candidates must be at least 40 years old and Estonian citizens.

The president's duties are mainly ceremonial, including representing Estonia in international relations and carrying out various diplomatic duties. The president is also responsible for initiating amendments to the constitution, declaring elections for the *Riigikogu,* and nominating candidates for prime minister.

A new constitution, based on that of 1938, was adopted following a referendum on June 28, 1992. The constitution guarantees equality before the law, regardless of sex, race, language, and political or religious beliefs.

POLITICAL PARTIES

There are currently 13 political parties represented in the *Riigikogu*. These include the ruling Estonian Coalition Party and Rural Union alliance, the Estonian Reform Party, the Estonian Center Party, the Fatherland alliance, the Moderates, the National Independence Party, the ethnic Russian Our Home is Estonia bloc, the Russian People's Party of Estonia, and the right-wing Republican People's Conservative Party.

For a party to be legally registered, it must have at least 1,000 members. In elections, a party must gain at least 5% of the total vote to be awarded any seats in the *Riigikogu*. Most of the larger political parties campaign on the basis of a complete economic and social program, while smaller parties, such as the ethnic Russian Our Home is Estonia bloc, represent the interests of a particular group or campaign on a single issue.

LOCAL GOVERNMENT

Under Soviet administration, there were no local governing bodies. Since independence, Estonia has introduced a system of local government that is still developing. Local government is divided into counties, towns, and rural municipalities. Local bodies are split into 15 *maakond* (counties) plus six cities: Tallinn, Tartu, Narva, Kohtla-Järve, Pärnu, and Sillamäe. Estonia practices a single-tier system of local government, with county councils acting as representatives of the national government at a regional level.

The local government carries out administrative functions, manages state property, and provides services. The increase of local government responsibilities has been severely hampered by lack of finances. Local government is funded by the national government. All Estonian citizens can vote in local elections, as can residents who are not citizens. However, only citizens can run for office.

JUSTICE

Justice is administered solely by Estonia's law courts. Rural and city courts hear cases at the local level. District courts can review the decisions of the lower courts, and the National Court, the highest court in the land, hears appeals. Judges are appointed for life by the president.

As in most democracies, all defendants are assumed innocent until proven guilty, and all defendants have the right to legal representation in court. The constitution provides that all court proceedings be held in public. Suspects can be held for 48 hours without being formally charged, while further detention requires a court order. Suspects can only be arrested with a warrant issued by a court.

Estonia's police force was formed in 1991 from the remnants of the Soviet militia and comes under the ministry of internal affairs.

The courthouse in Tallinn.

FOREIGN RELATIONS

Estonia, like the other Baltic states, has actively sought greater integration with Western Europe and is negotiating for membership in both the European Union and the North Atlantic Treaty Organization (NATO). Membership would help its economy and ensure Estonia's long-term security. Recent applications have failed although Estonia was accepted as an associate member of the European Union in 1995, giving it certain trading advantages and the possibility of full membership in the near future. In 1998 a United States-Baltic charter was formed, a step short of full NATO membership.

Estonia's relations with Moscow have been very fractious since independence. Following independence, Estonia's chief foreign policy aim was to ensure the swift withdrawal of all Soviet forces from Estonian soil. After long negotiations, withdrawal began in 1992 and was finally completed in September 1994. On a number of occasions Russia suspended the withdrawal to protest perceived discrimination against the Russian minority in Estonia.

Russia has expressed considerable disapproval at Estonia's attempts to join the Soviet Union's traditional adversary, NATO, and Estonia criticized Russia's 1995–96 military campaign in Chechnya. Anti-Baltic feeling is rife in Russia. In 1996 Russia's foreign minister Yevgeny Primakov suggested imposing economic sanctions on Estonia until the situation improved. Despite accusations of human rights abuses, international observer organizations could find no evidence to support the Russian claims. The Estonian government has offered social and civil guarantees to all retired Soviet military personnel living in Estonia to placate the Russians. In 1997, 19,000 Russian military retirees and their families were waiting for their residency applications to be processed. Russia's anti-Baltic rhetoric has led Estonia to view Russia as a serious security threat, with membership in NATO the only guarantee of Estonia's long-term security. NATO's sensitivity to Russian objections is likely to ensure that this will never happen. Russia still maintains a strong, intimidating military presence on the Estonian border, ostensibly to defend its western border and northern capital, St. Petersburg.

Estonia's relations with its Baltic and Scandinavian neighbors have been far more positive and productive. The Baltic Assembly was established in 1991 to provide a forum for discussions among the three Baltic countries; this was replaced by the Baltic Council in 1993. As a result of this cooperation, the Baltic countries sent a Baltic contingent to Bosnia as part of the peacekeeping force in 1995. Estonia has had particularly good relations with Sweden and Finland, which have played a crucial role in helping Estonia transform to a free-market democracy. Estonia's relationship with Finland is uniquely close and includes extensive cultural exchange as well as highly integrated economic and governmental ties. The Nordic countries are the largest donors of aid to the Baltic countries and have championed their interests in the international community. The Council of the Baltic Sea States, an organization that includes all the countries of the Baltic region (and notably the regional giants Russia and Germany), also offers the region a useful forum to discuss local issues and policy.

ARMED FORCES

Following the break-up of the Soviet Union, Estonia no longer had an army. Russia maintained a military presence in Estonia until the final withdrawal of its troops in 1994. In April 1992 Estonia established its own ministry of defense and an independent military. According to the constitution, the president is the supreme commander of the armed forces.

Estonia's total armed forces number around 3,500 men; most are in the army. Military service is for 12 months. Estonia also has some estimated 6,000 reserves, plus a paramilitary border guard of 2,000 men under the command of the ministry of the interior. Such a small force is no match for the Russian army, whose northern region forces alone number more than 50,000 and include extensive tank and aircraft support.

Estonia has increased cooperation with other Baltic countries, and a training center for the Baltic Battalion, the Baltic states' first joint military unit, was established in 1995 in Latvia.

Members of the Young Eagles, a youth military organization.

ECONOMY

OF ALL THE FORMER SOVIET STATES, Estonia embraced the free-market economy with the greatest enthusiasm and made the adjustment with the minimum of complications. Today, Estonia boasts one of the most successful post-communist economies in the world, with minimal government interference and no trade barriers. The state has strongly encouraged economic growth and foreign investment.

Historically, Estonia has always had an agricultural economy. Industrial development in the 1930s changed this, as did the forced collectivization of farms and further industrialization under the Soviets in the 1940s and 1950s. All property and industry were nationalized under Soviet rule. For 50 years Estonia's economy was centrally controlled and directed from Moscow as an integral part of the Soviet Union. Decisions concerning the country's economic and industrial development were made within the context of the whole USSR, and Estonia was totally subservient to Moscow's plans.

Estonia's transformation from a centrally controlled, Soviet-style economy to a free-market economy has been miraculously fast. Estonia began the transition to a market economy in the late 1980s with the establishment of a central bank and a private banking system. By mid-1994, only three years after independence, more than 50% of Estonia's gross domestic product (GDP) was being generated by the private sector.

This transformation has not occurred without some suffering for the Estonian people. The winter of 1991–92 was probably the hardest they have experienced since World War II, with the cost of living increasing tenfold over the year. This was particularly hard to bear, as Estonia had been one of the wealthiest regions in the USSR before independence. Much of this inflation was a result of having to pay world-market prices for essential goods when these materials had previously been provided at a subsidized cost as part of the Soviet-controlled economy.

Neatly piled timber stacks in readiness for winter in Estonia. Western companies have invested heavily in the Estonian timber industry.

TRADE

Estonia has a well-educated, technically skilled workforce and low wage rates compared to Western Europe, making the country very attractive to foreign investors. Companies from Europe and the United States have invested extensively in its timber, textile, and manufacturing industries. Estonia's neighbors, Sweden and Finland, have been two of its biggest investors and have purchased many of Estonia's newly privatized companies. Major American and Finnish corporations have also invested in the computer, electronics, and automobile industries.

Domestic trade is being rapidly developed from a relatively narrow base. The Estonian economy enjoys an export-led boom. Estonia exports goods chiefly to Finland, Sweden, Russia, Latvia, and Germany. Estonia's main sources of imported goods are Finland, Russia, Germany, and Sweden. At one time 70% of Estonia's trade was with the Russian Federation, but this has dropped to around 15% as Estonia's trade links with the West grow. In 1997 around 65% of Estonian trade was with

countries of the European Union—50% with Finland and Sweden alone. Estonia has free trade agreements with the Baltic states, Finland, Sweden, Norway, the European Union, Switzerland, and the Ukraine. For much of the 1990s, poor relations with Russia deprived Estonia of preferential access to Russian markets. Recently Russia has softened its attitude toward Estonia, and a new ambassador has been appointed to Tallinn, indicating a thaw in political and economic relations.

Container ships in the harbor at Tallinn, evidence of Estonia's flourishing international trade.

FINANCE

Estonia was the first former Soviet republic to introduce its own currency, the kroon, in June 1992. The kroon has proved to be a remarkably strong and stable currency and has delivered Estonia from the raging inflation that existed when the Russian ruble was still in use.

Average earnings in Estonia are US$4,000 (1997) per year, while the economy grew at a rate of almost 10% in 1997. Inflation, though high at 11% in 1997, has steadily decreased throughout the 1990s.

AGRICULTURE AND INDUSTRY

Approximately 70,000 Estonians are employed in the agricultural sector —less than 8% of the workforce. Combined with fishing, agriculture contributes only 10% of total industrial output. This is in marked contrast to Estonia's traditional role as a rural, agrarian economy.

For centuries, Estonians referred to themselves as *Maarahvas* ("MAH-ruh-vuhs"), meaning "people of the land." Over the centuries, the farming lifestyle became a part of the Estonian identity. In the 1930s—the heyday of Estonian agriculture—it was popularly thought that Estonian eggs, butter, and meat graced the breakfast tables of St. Petersburg and London.

Opposite: **Corrugated iron silos outside a commercial farm.**

Below: **Dairy farming produces the country's chief agricultural products: meat, milk, and butter.**

In the Soviet era, Estonia's farms were forcibly collectivized and brought under government control. Many traditional family farms were lost, and many farmers were deported to Siberia for resisting the collectivization. By 1949 Estonia's 140,000 farms had been converted into 2,400 state-run units. In the 1990s the process has been reversed, with farms being privatized, reorganized, and reinstated to their former family-run status. Inefficiency remains a problem for Estonia's farms, and farmers have difficulty financing the purchase of modern farming equipment. Consequently, overall agricultural production has steadily declined through the 1990s, and many farmers struggle to do more than break even. In 1996 it was estimated that a quarter of the rural population was unemployed because of this decline. This downward trend is slowly reversing as reorganization takes effect and efficiency improves.

Barley, grains, potatoes, and other vegetables are the principal crops grown. Dairy farms are numerous, and meat, milk, eggs, and butter are the country's chief agricultural products. Combined with fishing, dairy products contribute 57% of the food industry's total output. Estonia's food processing industry meets domestic demand.

ECONOMY

Hard at work in the oil-shale mines.

FORESTRY Estonia's forests, which cover 40% of the country, are an obvious natural resource. The exploitation of these forests provides timber for furniture manufacturing, pulp plants, paper goods, and fuel.

Estonians' timber skills and low wage levels have made the timber industry highly competitive and successful. The timber industry contributes 12% of total industrial output and is considered the country's most promising industry.

ENGINEERING AND ELECTRONICS Estonia's engineering and electronics industry has grown rapidly since independence, fueled by extensive foreign investment. The machinery and electronics industry led Estonian exports in 1995, and contributes 12% to total industrial output. Products include electronic motors, integrated circuits, cables, and other high-tech products. Factories formerly working for the Soviet military have been successfully adapted to sell to Western markets.

TEXTILES Estonia's thriving textile industry has adjusted quickly to the demands of a market economy. Estonia exports clothing and footwear products to Europe and the United States. The textile industry contributes 12% of total industrial output.

CHEMICALS Estonia has large phosphorite deposits, which are the basis of a fertilizer manufacturing industry. The chemical industry contributes more than 10% of Estonia's industrial output, including oil-shale, household chemical products, fertilizers, plastics, paints, and lacquer products.

ENERGY

In the past Estonia was heavily dependent on Soviet energy supplies. Since independence the oil-shale industry, centered around Kohtla-Järve, Kiviõli, and Narva, has become Estonia's main source of domestic and industrial energy, providing 14% of industrial output. Estonia has abundant supplies of oil-shale, estimated at 16.5 billion tons (15 billion tonnes). Most of the oil-shale is used to supply thermal power plants to generate electricity, much of which is exported to Latvia and Russia.

Peat and firewood are also significant energy sources, as are two hydroelectric plants on the Narva River. The government is actively seeking ways to upgrade the thermal power plants to control pollution and limit damage to the environment.

The town of Kiviõli, in Estonia's industrial northeast, has the dubious distinction of having the country's highest ash hill at 380 feet (116 m).

An oil-shale power station in Kohtla-Järve.

SERVICES AND TOURISM

Most urban Estonians make a trip to the country every summer. Southern Estonia and the islands are the most popular rural destinations, while Pärnu is the most visited city.

Estonia's service industry is the best developed in the former Soviet Union and is one of the country's biggest growth industries. Tourism is growing, and since 1990 has been coordinated by the National Tourist Board. Foreigners and local residents visit the historic towns of Tallinn and Tartu and experience the tranquillity of the rural interior or the coastal resorts and islands of Hiiumaa and Saaremaa.

It is estimated that 2.5 million foreigners visited Estonia in 1997, producing nearly 15% of its GDP earnings. The vast majority of these visitors were from neighboring Finland while others came from Latvia, Russia, and Sweden. Ferries have been crossing the Gulf of Finland since 1936, and many Finns take day-trips on cruise ships from Helsinki to Tallinn to see the sights of the Estonian capital. Since independence, there has been a rapid increase in bed-and-breakfast establishments and home stays organized by Western travel agents.

THE ESTONIAN FERRY DISASTER

On September 28, 1994, the Estonian passenger ferry *Estonia* capsized off the coast of Finland, killing 859 people in Europe's worst postwar shipping disaster. The ferry was en route from Tallinn to Stockholm with 1,040 passengers and crew when it encountered strong gales and waves 33 feet (10 m) high. Water flooded the car deck. The weight of the water and the unchained vehicles caused the ferry to list heavily to one side, and eventually sink at 2 a.m.

A great mystery surrounds the cause of the tragedy. The official report suggests that weak locks and the faulty design of the bow doors caused them to be forced open in the bad weather and rolling seas, letting water into the car deck. However, the German builders of the ferry reject the official findings. Conspiracy theories are rife, suggesting that the *Estonia* was carrying a smuggled cargo of narcotics or a consignment of high-tech military equipment. Poor seamanship or bad design are the most likely causes, but as yet, no definitive explanation has been discovered.

TRANSPORTATION

Estonia has good road and rail links with Russia and other parts of the Commonwealth of Independent States, built in the Soviet period. This makes trade and communication with commonwealth countries easy, and allows Estonia to act as a bridge between the Baltic countries and Russia and beyond into the Central Asian republics. Estonia has a 630-mile (1,015-km) comprehensive rail system that links all of the country's main towns and industrial centers.

Estonia's 9,000 miles (14,500 km) of roads are more than adequate for its small population and low volume of traffic. A massive highway, the Via Baltika, is being constructed through the three Baltic countries, in the hope that it will one day be the main link between Eastern and Central Europe and Finland and northern Russia.

Estonia's ports are vital to the country's transportation system, providing a historic gateway from Western Europe that leads deep into Russia and beyond into other former Soviet republics.

Tallinn's transportation network is the most advanced in the country.

Estonia's national airline, Estonian Air, began operating in 1992. Tallinn is served by direct air links with Stockholm, Amsterdam, Frankfurt, London, Warsaw, Moscow, Kiev, Vilnius, and Copenhagen.

ESTONIANS

ESTONIA IS A MULTICULTURAL COUNTRY of less than 1.5 million people. Ethnic Estonians make up 64% of the population, while ethnic Russians are the second largest group at 29%. The other major ethnic groups in Estonia are much smaller: Ukrainians (2.7%), Belorussians (1.6%), and Finns (1%). Other minorities include Tatars, Jews, Latvians, Poles, Lithuanians, and Germans.

The ethnic mixture of people in Estonia has changed drastically over the last 50 years, as a result of the Baltic country's incorporation into the Soviet Union and consequent Soviet migration policies. In the last five decades, Estonia has become the home of more than 100 different ethnic groups, mainly from other parts of the Soviet Union. In 1934 a census showed that 88% of the people in Estonia were ethnic Estonians. In the 1990s, that figure had fallen by more than a quarter, while the number of Russians dramatically increased from a pre-1940 figure of 8% to nearly a third of the population today. Between 1945 and 1990, approximately 1.4 million mostly Russian-speaking peoples passed through Estonia. Such a dense flow of people has had a corrosive effect on traditional Estonian society and has led to domestic tensions. Today, it has been estimated that a quarter of the country's residents were born outside of the country.

The population of Estonia has dropped through the 1990s. According to a 1989 census, the population was 1,565,000; by 1997 the number had fallen to 1,464,000. This decrease is mainly a result of a halt in migration from the former Soviet Union and a drop in the birth rate. It is estimated that as many as 80,000 people have left Estonia since 1991. While some have migrated to the West, many have returned to their homeland.

Estonia has a low population density. Despite being a bigger country than, for example, Switzerland, Estonia has only one quarter of the population.

Opposite: **Two boys sit atop Toompea Hill, looking out over Tallinn.**

Young Estonians come from all over the country to visit the capital. Here, three girls pose for a photograph in front of Tallinn's city wall.

ESTONIANS

Estonians are a Finno-Ugric people, one among an ethno-linguistic group that includes the Finns, Lapps, and Hungarians. They first arrived in Estonia around 6,000 B.C., having journeyed across the Asian landmass from the marshes of Siberia.

Estonians are not related to their Baltic neighbors, the Latvians and Lithuanians, who are Indo-European peoples. Ethnically and culturally, Estonians are close cousins to Finns and have more in common with them than with the other Baltic peoples. Estonians feel themselves to be very Scandinavian and not at all linked to Slavic peoples.

Estonians are traditionally a rural people. In Estonia today, the rural areas are totally dominated by native Estonians, many of whom still pursue the traditional vocations of farming, forestry, and fishing. On Saaremaa and Hiiumaa, 95% of the people are Estonians. The ethnic minorities tend to predominate in the industrial towns and cities. Among the cities, Tartu is rare in being predominantly Estonian in ethnic makeup and character.

CHARACTERISTICS

Estonians are typical northern Europeans in that they are extremely individualistic and love solitude. It is said that Estonians are happiest when their nearest neighbor is at least a mile away! This explains the popularity of country homes: in the summer, most Estonians like to retreat to their country houses for as long as possible. The Baltic peoples are generally passive in character and not given to great displays of passion or affection. Visitors find Estonians cool and reserved—almost frighteningly so—and say they have mastered the art of being polite without being friendly. The Slavic peoples, especially the Russians, tend to be more expansive and openly affectionate, offering hugs to each other when meeting. Estonians shy away from open displays of affection and tend to negatively associate this behavior with their least favorite neighbor. For Estonians, friendship is highly prized and not easily proffered.

Enjoying the sunshine on a summer's day.

THE ESTONIAN IDENTITY

Estonians have been a self-aware nation for only 100 years or so, following the nationalist revival of the late 19th century. For Estonians, ethnic identity is the essence of their nationhood. Domination by foreign powers is most apparent in the architecture of the country, which is mainly German, Swedish, and Russian in character. Many Estonian institutions were also introduced by these conquerors. Consequently, Estonians have retained a sense of themselves through their traditions, language, and lifestyle. As a part of the Soviet Union, Estonians were not allowed to express their separateness or celebrate their culture and were instead encouraged to adhere to the Communist Party ideal of the Soviet citizen—a "universal" human dedicated to international socialism. This ideology never appealed to the individualistic Estonians.

As a result of nationalistic feeling, Estonians have turned resolutely toward the West to find a new lifestyle and sense of purpose; one not dominated by Russia and communist ideology.

DRESS

As a result of their newfound affluence, Estonians dress much like people elsewhere in the West. Long gone are the days of drab, Soviet-style suits. Western-made designer clothes can be bought in many shops in Tallinn. Clothes from nearby Finland and Sweden are also popular. The long winters and cold weather mean that warm clothing is the norm; this includes heavy coats, sweaters, scarves, heavy boots, and thick socks.

Though there are regional variations, Estonians do have a recognizable national dress. Today, it is often worn on festive occasions, especially for summer song festivals. Since independence, wearing traditional dress has become increasingly popular at national celebrations as a way of visibly expressing Estonian culture. Women dress in long, heavy, woven skirts, gathered at the waist. The skirts are usually red, black, yellow, or orange and decorated with either fine vertical stripes or wide horizontal bands. White, long-sleeved blouses are usually worn above the skirts, with wide, lace-edged collars and cuffs. The blouses are sometimes embroidered with floral designs and motifs. The collar is often fastened with a large, ornamental pin.

Female folk singers dressed in traditional clothes.

Sleeveless bodices are also worn. If a skirt with vertical stripes is worn, it is usually combined with a heavy apron of the same shade. A black belt holds the apron and skirt in place. The outfit is usually worn with white stockings and black shoes. Women often wear close-fitting caps made of white linen and decorated with lace and silk ribbons.

Estonian men wear black breeches, fastened at the knees with silver buttons, with a patterned vest over a white, long-sleeved shirt. The shirt is fastened at the neck with a braided tie or pin. Sometimes, a skullcap is worn on the head. Similar to the women, white stockings and black shoes are also worn.

RUSSIANS

Russians make up 29% of Estonia's population. A similar situation exists in neighboring Latvia, where Russians are one-third of the population. Some Russians have lived in the Baltic countries since the 18th century, after Russia annexed the region from Sweden in the Great Northern War.

In Estonia, most of these early migrants lived in villages around Lake Peipus. The vast majority of today's Russians moved to Estonia during the Soviet occupation—some were encouraged to move as administrators in the Soviet government, while others moved to work in the industries of Estonia's northeast. Today Russians are a highly visible presence in the industrial towns of northern Estonia. In Narva 98% of the people are ethnic Russians, while Kohtla-Järve and Sillamäe have mainly Russian populations. As a result, the historically Estonian region of Ida-Virumaa has taken on a very Russian character. Even in the capital, Tallinn, half the population is Russian. Only about 40% of Estonia's Russian population were born in Estonia. Many retired Russian military personnel, especially officers, have chosen to remain in Estonia.

A Russian dairy farmer waits for the ferry to Tallinn.

Since independence, the presence of the large Russian minority has caused problems. Russians without Estonian citizenship claim they are discriminated against in the workplace or treated as second-class citizens regarding salaries and public housing. Many perceived injustices have been reported in the Russian press and are a source of tension between Estonia and Russia. However, a majority of Russians questioned in a Moscow-based report in 1994 denied discrimination.

Unfortunately, a linguistic barrier still exists and hinders full integration. For 50 years Russian was the lingua franca of the whole Soviet Union, and the Russians in Estonia did not need to learn to speak Estonian. Today a knowledge of Estonian is essential for education, business, and citizenship. Consequently, some Russians feel disadvantaged and alienated.

Independence has had some positive effects for the minority peoples. It has allowed them the opportunity to rediscover their own ethnic identity, as well as to learn more about the history, language, and culture of Estonia.

OTHER PEOPLES

Before Soviet rule, many people from neighboring countries lived in Estonia, such as Swedes, Germans, Latvians, and Finns. These peoples had historical and cultural links with Estonia and were generally part of a small, educated elite.

Today's minorities are chiefly Slavic peoples who migrated from the former Soviet Union. Apart from Russians, there are significant numbers of Ukrainians and Belorussians in Estonia. Along with people from Azerbaijan, Armenia, Moldova, the Soviet Far East, and Siberia, these settlers were recruited by the government in Moscow to work in the construction, oil-shale, and power industries in the 1950s, 1960s, and 1970s. Separated from their homeland and discouraged from learning about Estonian culture, most non-Russians melted into the Russian-speaking population, learning Russian and sending their children to Russian-language schools. Consequently, in post-independence Estonia these people had difficulties assimilating with native Estonians.

The other major groups in Estonia are Jews, Latvians, Poles, Germans, and Lithuanians. The Latvians live mainly in the rural areas near the Latvian border.

In 1993 the Estonian government introduced the Law of Cultural Autonomy, giving all minorities the legal right to preserve and celebrate their identity, language, and culture. In 1995 there were no fewer than 60 separate ethnic societies promoting minority peoples—many funded by the government. Many are housed in the Estonian Nationalities Club in

Tallinn, where cultural promotion and social activities are given priority. Orchestras have been developed and handicraft groups formed, as well as choirs. The Slavic Cultural and Charity Society has revived traditional Russian song and dance festivals. The government hopes that those ethnic groups who choose to remain will integrate to form a multicultural element in Estonia.

FINNO-UGRIC PEOPLES Finno-Ugric peoples—such as the Mordvinians, Karelians, Udmurts, and Maris—also moved to Estonia as part of Soviet migration policies in the 1960s and 1970s. They came from areas west of the Ural Mountains and near the Volga River in Russia and are related to the Estonians by ancient linguistic and ethnic ties. Today, Finno-Ugric peoples number around 3,000.

ESTONIAN SWEDES Estonian Swedes have traditionally lived along the northwest coast of the country, around Haapsalu and on the islands. Before the Soviet occupation, there were as many as 7,000 Swedes living in Estonia. Most fled the advancing Russian army in 1944. Now there are only 300 or so Swedes in the country.

THE SETUS

The Setus are a small group of Finno-Ugric people who inhabit the formerly disputed Russian area around the city of Pechory southeast of Estonia. The Setus have ancient ethnic and traditional ties with Estonians. In the Middle Ages the Setus came under the control of the Russian principality of Pskov and the region has been occupied by Russian troops for most of the time since. Over the centuries, the Setus drifted away from their Estonian counterparts and absorbed more Slavic culture and traditions, while Estonians were heavily influenced by German and Swedish culture. Consequently, the Setus have a mixed Estonian-Russian culture. Most Setus are Russian Orthodox Christians and speak a dialect of the Võru tongue, common in southeastern Estonia.

LIFESTYLE

ON THE EVE OF INDEPENDENCE, Estonians could boast of having the highest per capita income and the most generous housing allocation in the whole Soviet Union. The immediate aftermath of independence made life much tougher for many Estonians, creating high unemployment, food and fuel shortages, poorer services, and general uncertainty during the transition to a free-market economy and self-rule.

Today the gap between the rich and the poor continues to widen, as those who have prospered in the free-market economy leave the disadvantaged and unemployed behind. Overall, however, shortages are a thing of the past, and many Estonians can afford goods and vacations that were previously beyond their reach. Despite some outstanding problems, Estonia is now a happier, more prosperous, and confident place than in the early 1990s, and Estonians are in control of their own destiny.

Left: **Relaxing in Tallinn's town square.**

Opposite: **Visitors wait in line to enter the famous Alexander Nevsky Cathedral.**

CITY LIFE

Many city dwellers have summer houses in the country, or at least an allotment of land on the outskirts of their city. Estonians' strong identification with nature and a love of solitude take them to their country cottages every summer in search of rural tranquillity. Gardening is popular, and many people take great pride in their gardens.

More than 70% of Estonians live in towns or cities. The center of Tallinn is still a pleasant place to live, with historic architecture, picturesque towers, and cobbled streets. The number of places to eat and drink in Tallinn has greatly improved since the Soviet era, when restaurants were few and service generally poor. Now, most streets in the capital have some place to eat or drink. Cellar bars and cafés are very popular in urban areas, and provide warm and cozy retreats from the winter weather. However, they are considered too hot and stuffy in the summer, a time Estonians prefer to be outdoors, in the countryside if possible. Nightclubs are also popular in Tallinn.

The goods in Estonian shop windows are beginning to compare favorably with those in Scandinavia and include chic fashions, especially in Tallinn. The Scandinavian influence is also apparent in the appearance of clothing stores in the capital. Western-style boutiques and barber shops are also increasingly common.

The riches of the free-market economy are still only enjoyed by a small percentage of the population. Tenement blocks ring most of Estonia's major cities, a leftover from the Soviet era. Tallinn Old Town seems a world away from the drab housing developments of Õisemäe and Mustamäe south of the city. Many of Estonia's Russian minority live in these high-rise suburbs. Overcrowding is a problem, with parents plus two children squeezed into a one-bedroom apartment. Electricity and water supplies are often unreliable. There is still high unemployment in some urban areas, especially the cities of Narva, Kohtla-Järve, and Sillamäe. The living standard in these cities is poor because of the horrendous pollution that characterizes the northeast of the country and causes increased health problems, especially lung and heart disease.

Opposite: **Most Estonians with a piece of land will grow some crops or garden vegetables.**

66

COUNTRY LIFE

About a third of Estonia's population lives in the rural areas, almost all of them ethnic Estonians. Estonians feel themselves to be essentially country people. Following independence, many rural Estonians wished to return to the prewar idyll of the self-sufficient smallholder. The state-run collective farms were swiftly replaced by family-run farms that blossomed in the hands of their new owners.

Rural Estonians are far more traditional and less exposed to outside influences—not many speak a foreign language, apart from Russian. Creature comforts are fewer in the country. People put in long, hard hours of manual labor and suffer the physical privations that come with long, cold, and dark winters. Some houses do not have running hot water or central heating and wood is often stacked in neat piles around the house for fuel. Off the main highways, unpaved, dusty country roads lack proper road markings or signs. Unlike the cities, shops, businesses, and restaurants tend to close at 5 p.m., and everything is closed on Sunday. These inconveniences are offset by the advantages of breathing clean air, having plenty of space, and being able to indulge in picking wild flowers, berries, and mushrooms.

Two young children fishing off a dock. Estonia has never had a baby boom, though the number of births did peak in the late 1980s, but has since fallen sharply.

FAMILY AND MARRIAGE

Estonians have developed a liberal, easygoing attitude toward sex and marriage. More than 80% of first births are conceived out of wedlock, with more than half born out of wedlock.

Estonia has for many decades had a low birth rate. The population increased mainly because of the arrival of immigrants from other parts of the Soviet Union. With immigration halted since independence, the population is steadily declining. Abortion is common, with the number of abortions each year outpacing the number of births. Child care and child rearing have become expensive since independence, so couples prefer a small family to increase their standard of living.

There has been a decline in the number of people marrying in Estonia in recent years. More than half of couples live together before getting married, and many continue to cohabit without marrying. Divorce is increasingly common and usually initiated by women. This has led to quite a diversity of lifestyles in Estonia, with both the traditional extended family and two-parent family being less common than in the past. Unlike their Latvian neighbors, marriages between ethnic Estonians and Russians and other minorities are comparatively rare.

Traditional marriage practices have also declined in Estonia. This is partly a result of 50 years of Soviet policies and partly because few Estonians practice religion.

HOSPITALITY

Estonians are not known for their outward friendliness, and unlike their fellow Baltics, the Lithuanians and Latvians, do not invite people they barely know to their homes. Estonians are not truly selfish or unfriendly, but they value friendship highly and do not offer invitations lightly.

A happy couple with their young child.

Estonians normally greet each other with a handshake, and some men may tip their hats. Offering cut flowers when visiting is universal for any kind of gathering, celebration, or party, and always proves a popular gift. Flower shops are found on nearly every street corner in towns and cities.

When Estonians entertain at home, it is usually to share a meal and drinks with family and close friends. Estonians are at their most relaxed when gathered around a table. Alcohol often features prominently. Drinking alcohol is a popular way of relaxing in Estonia, as it is throughout Scandinavia and the Baltics. Cheap alcohol is one of the chief reasons many Finns like to visit Tallinn for day or weekend trips. In 1997 an underground pipeline was discovered under the Latvia-Estonia border, believed to be used to smuggle bootleg vodka from Latvia, where it is cheaper!

AN AGING POPULATION

Life expectancy for Estonian men is 66, and for women 75, figures that have changed very little since the 1960s. A high proportion of ethnic Estonians are over 60 years old (one in five), and trends suggest Estonia will support an increasingly elderly population. Before independence, young immigrants arrived from other parts of the Soviet Union. As a result, there is a greater proportion of young people among the ethnic minorities. The long decline in fertility rates has also contributed to a disproportionately aging population.

In the past not enough attention was paid to providing housing and services for the older generation. Now the government has had to invest in housing, social services, medical care, and transportation for this group. This need has placed severe demands on a developing and overstretched economy.

Many of Estonia's older generation live in their own houses or apartments.

EDUCATION

According to the constitution, education is compulsory for all school-age children. While much of the education system is being gradually restructured for the needs of the new republic, Estonia has kept many of the old Soviet institutions intact. In recent years, there have been difficulties recruiting people into a profession perceived to be low-paying in an industry that is underfunded. As a consequence, classroom shortages have become common, and teachers have gone on strike to protest staff shortages and poor conditions.

The University of Tartu, Estonia's first university, was established by the Swedes in the 17th century. The language of instruction was Swedish, later to be replaced by Russian. Estonian was only introduced as the language of instruction in 1919, following independence. In the Soviet period, emphasis was placed on learning Russian (though Estonian was also taught), and the syllabus was heavily politicized.

Today the goal of the education system is to promote Estonian language and culture. Most schools are run by the state, though private schools are slowly being introduced.

ELEMENTARY AND SECONDARY SCHOOLS   It is compulsory for children to attend elementary and secondary school, beginning at age 7. Students are obliged to stay in school until they have completed their basic education or until they are 17. There are more than 700 secondary schools in Estonia.

Lessons are taught in either Estonian (roughly 70%) or Russian. Students are also required to learn at least two foreign languages. The most popular choices are English, German, Russian, Finnish, and French.

At Tartu University there is a famous sacrificial stone where students, having adapted a pagan custom, ritually burn their notebooks at midnight on the Thursday before their exams.

WOMEN AT WORK

In general, women have adapted more easily to changes in lifestyle and work in post-independence Estonia than men. Women have found it easier to develop the skills needed in the new workplace, such as dealing graciously with strangers. However, there is still considerable institutionalized inequality. Although Estonian women are legally entitled to equal pay at work,

in reality they are paid less despite having an average higher educational level than their male counterparts. Traditional thinking that regards men as the chief breadwinner still dominates in Estonia and is taken for granted by many employers. Estonian women tend to work in traditional female professions. For example, they are the majority of secondary schoolteachers (83%), while there are only 12 women in the 101-seat state assembly. Women make up more than half of the working population. They also do most of the household chores and look after the children, despite their work commitments.

Although the government encourages the teaching of minority cultures and languages, financial constraints have made the establishment of minority schools difficult. A few private Russian, Swedish, and Jewish schools do exist.

COLLEGES There are 13 public and eight private institutions of higher education. College education lasts four to six years. There are six universities, with more than 25,000 students: Tartu University, Tallinn Technical University, Estonian Academy of Arts, Tallinn Music Academy, Estonian Agricultural University, and Tallinn Pedagogical University. Tartu University is Estonia's oldest and biggest university with more than 8,000 students. It has the largest library in Estonia, which owns the first book written in Estonian—a prayer book published in 1525. There are seven vocational institutions that teach practical and technical subjects such as business management, navigation, aviation, and tourism, with more than 27,000 students. Most college courses are taught in Estonian, and students who wish to continue their education in Russian generally complete their studies in Russia. There are a number of private institutions, including the American-run Concordia International University in Tallinn where the syllabus concentrates on practical subjects such as business studies and communications, and classes are taught in English.

WELFARE

As a part of the Soviet Union, health care and welfare were provided and funded by the state. This system has been gradually restructured in the 1990s, with the introduction of new pension and unemployment plans. Although unemployment was high at the beginning of the 1990s, especially in the rural areas and in the industrial northeast, in 1997 it was down to the manageable level of 3.5%. Consequently, most government social security spending is for old age and retirement pensions. In 1994 a minimum income was guaranteed to all Estonian families. Free medical care is provided for all school-age children.

Estonia's publicly run hospitals are gradually improving, though financial constraints have slowed progress. A system of medical insurance has been introduced, while limited medical care is free for everyone.

Statistics show that there are 35 physicians and 90 beds per 10,000 inhabitants. Private hospitals and clinics exist but only the wealthy can afford them. Many of these are foreign-run, often by Finns.

A baby being treated at a clinic. Clinics in every town and most large villages provide basic medical care. County and town hospitals offer more specialized care.

RELIGION

AT THE MERCY OF SHIFTING SPHERES of influence, modern Estonia has been left a legacy of churches and faiths, ranging from Lutheranism through Catholicism, Orthodoxy, Judaism, and Islam. For nearly 500 years Lutheranism, a Protestant religion, has been Estonia's official faith. Despite a nominal adherence to the Lutheran Church, Estonians are (and have always been) one of the most secular people in Europe. Today only 23% of Estonians claim to have any religious convictions (though the figure is higher among ethnic Russians, who tend to follow the Orthodox faith).

The government has associated itself with the Lutheran Church as part of its nation-building program, and religious studies have been reintroduced into the public school curriculum as an optional subject. Historically, there has been considerable tolerance of other churches and faiths, and freedom of religious practice and belief is guaranteed under the constitution.

Left: **A tapestry depicting Martin Luther delivering a sermon to members of the dukedom who supported his drive for religious reform in the 16th century.**

Opposite: **The Duomo of Tallinn.**

ANCIENT PRACTICES

Estonians' ancient cosmogony is still preserved in folkloric traditions. Before the forced conversion of Estonians to Christianity by the German Crusaders, animistic beliefs held sway along the Baltic coast. Trees, rocks, hills, fields, and animals were worshiped as powerful spiritual forces. Much of this pagan religion was a product of the lifestyle of a hunter-fisher society at a time when trees covered most of Estonia.

Forests were thought to contain powerful spirits that could cause those who had behaved badly—especially those who damaged the forest—to lose their way or be attacked by forest animals. Springs, rivers, and lakes were also believed to contain spirits that could injure or kill the unwary. Spirits could be both protective and dangerous forces. The dead were also thought to inhabit the world as spirits and could be called on for assistance through funeral rites and sacrifices.

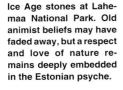

Ice Age stones at Lahemaa National Park. Old animist beliefs may have faded away, but a respect and love of nature remains deeply embedded in the Estonian psyche.

THE EVANGELICAL LUTHERAN CHURCH

Protestant Lutheranism—the dominant religion of most of Scandinavia and northern Germany—has been Estonia's official religion since it replaced Catholicism following the Reformation in 1520. Because of continuing warfare, however, the Lutheran Church developed slowly in Estonia, remaining a superficial influence until the establishment of a state church by Swedish rulers in the 17th century. Estonians were unable to gain direct access to the teachings of the Church until an Estonian edition of the New Testament was published in 1686, making religion more accessible to common people. A full translation of the Bible was written in 1739, and religion was taught in newly established schools.

Lutheran practices suffered during the Tsarist years because of the states' overt promotion of the Orthodox Church. But in 1919 the church was reorganized and renamed the Estonian Evangelical Lutheran Church, for the first time coming under Estonian control. In Estonia's first period of independence (1920–40), the Lutheran Church flourished and 80% of

Estonia's first churches were built on the islands in the early 13th century, following the conquest by German Crusaders. They were simple structures, without towers, and were used chiefly for defense. Many of Estonia's pre-Reformation churches were decorated by local and foreign artists.

SACRED TREES

As a result of Estonian ancient religious practices and the people's love of nature, there are many sacred trees in Estonia today. In ancient times Estonians would gather under oak trees before making important decisions. Estonia's most famous sacred tree—the Pühajärv Oak—decorates the country's ten-kroon banknote. Standing 65 feet (20 m) tall between a cow pasture and a lake, it is believed to be the oldest and biggest oak in the country. In 1841, this famous oak became the site of unrest when peasants fought their German landlords over harsh and exploitative working conditions.

Opposite: **Alexander Nevsky Cathedral. In the 1920s, during Estonia's first period of independence, it was suggested that the cathedral be modified and used for more practical purposes. The cathedral survived the threat and is now the center of Russian Orthodoxy in Tallinn.**

the population were officially listed as members. Following the Soviet occupation in 1945, religious worship was discouraged by the atheist communist state. Two-thirds of Estonia's clergy disappeared in the early years, and many churches were confiscated or closed down. By the 1970s less than 10% of Estonians were prepared to publicly claim adherence to Christianity. In the late 1980s, during the liberating effect of *glasnost,* the repressive legislation was lifted. There was a surge of interest in the Lutheran Church. The Church allied itself to the burgeoning independence movement, and Estonians wanted to express their newfound freedom by celebrating everything Estonian. Briefly, baptisms rose tenfold, although this initial enthusiasm has since waned. There are approximately 200 Lutheran congregations in the country today.

Lutheran practice is far more austere than that of the Catholic and Orthodox faiths. The preaching of sermons plays an essential role in the service, as does the singing of hymns. Lutherans observe just two sacraments: baptism and the Lord's Supper (Communion). Church rites include confirmation, ordination, marriage, and burial. Confirmation is normally given between the ages of 10 and 15, and includes a baptism and public profession of the faith by the recipient.

THE ORTHODOX CHURCH

The Russian Orthodox Church was officially established in the 18th century following Estonia's absorption into Tsarist Russia. Promoted by the Russian bureaucracy, Orthodoxy had moderate success, due in part to the peasants' desire to find an alternative to Lutheranism, perceived to be the religion of the German landlords. In the 19th century Orthodox membership rose as high as 20%.

Tsar Alexander III (1860–96) commissioned the construction of Orthodox churches throughout Estonia. The Alexander Nevsky Cathedral, built in the 1890s, is the most famous of these and stands on Toompea Hill in the center of Tallinn.

The status of the Orthodox Church has recently been a source of friction between Russia and Estonia. Following the restoration of independence in 1991, negotiations were held between the Constantinople and Moscow Patriarchs over the status of Estonia's Orthodox communities, the majority of whom wanted to return to Constantinople's jurisdiction. No agreement was reached, and in 1996 the Constantinople Patriarch decided to restore the Estonian Church to its jurisdiction. The Russian religious authorities viewed this as yet another

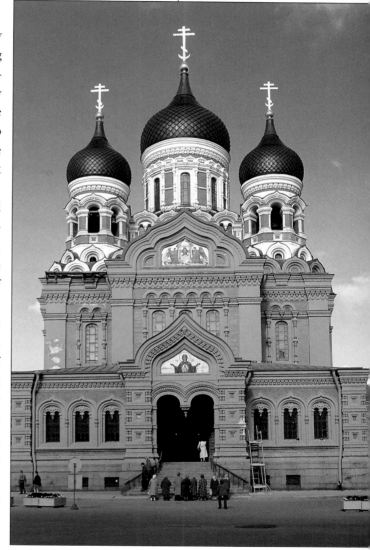

slight and act of defiance on the part of Estonia and temporarily suspended relations with the Constantinople Patriarch. The dispute has recently been resolved, and the Estonian government has guaranteed freedom of worship to the predominantly Russian congregations that wish to remain under the jurisdiction of the Moscow Patriarch.

Of the more than 80 Orthodox congregations in Estonia today, 25 are Russian and 10 are Old Believer. Ritual is an important part of worship for Russian Orthodox churches and includes music, the burning of incense, and chanting. Icons are positioned around the inside of most churches, and walls are covered with frescoes depicting religious events and symbolizing religious ideas. Believers pray in front of the icons, lighting candles as offerings and often kissing the icons as a sign of respect and supplication. The combined experience is intended to convey the mysterious essence of the faith. In contrast, Estonia's Orthodox churches and services are typically austere in character and lack the colorful decoration and pageant of their Russian counterparts.

OTHER CHRISTIAN CHURCHES

Other Christian churches, such as the Baptists, Methodists, and Seventh-Day Adventists, have been growing in popularity in Estonia. There are an estimated 5,000 practicing Catholics in Estonia, many of whom come from Estonia's Polish, Ukrainian, and Lithuanian minorities. The Baptist and Methodist churches have proved popular with some Estonians, who have sought new forms of Christian worship outside the Lutheran and Orthodox faiths and their historically negative associations. Jehovah's Witnesses and Mormon congregations also flourish.

OTHER RELIGIONS

Many non-Christian religions are practiced in Estonia today, chiefly by ethnic minorities who came to Estonia during the Soviet period. Additionally, the more mystical elements in Estonian traditional religion have contributed to the rising popularity of holistic religions, such as the Hare Krishna.

JUDAISM Until World War II, there was a large Jewish population throughout the Baltic region. However, Baltic Jews were heavily persecuted by the Nazis—hundreds of thousands were deported and killed—and Estonia was triumphantly declared "Judenfrei" (free of Jews). Since the War a small Jewish population has reestablished itself. There are approximately 4,000 Jews living in Estonia today, mainly in and around Tallinn, where there is a synagogue.

ISLAM Estonia has very few Muslims; most arrived in the country to work on industrial projects during the Soviet period. Estonia's Muslims are mainly from the former Soviet republics of the Caucasus region and Central Asia, and include Azerbaijanis, Ossetians, and Uzbeks.

Baptist churches first appeared in Estonia at the end of the 19th century, and were soon followed by the arrival of the Seventh-Day Adventists.

LANGUAGE

ESTONIAN IS THE NATIONAL LANGUAGE of Estonia and is spoken as a mother tongue by almost all ethnic Estonians. Russian, Ukrainian, Belorussian, and Finnish are also widely spoken by the larger ethnic minorities in Estonia, while to a lesser extent, German, Latvian, Lithuanian, Polish, Swedish, and Tatar are also spoken.

Since independence, language has become a highly politicized issue in Estonia. All citizens are required to speak the national language to a minimal level, regardless of their mother tongue. Consequently, Estonian has been introduced as the primary means of instruction in schools, mainly with the long-term aim of integrating non-Estonians into society. In 1995 the government passed a law that permits local government administrative procedures in districts with a non-Estonian majority to be conducted in a minority language. In practice this would mean Russian in much of the northeast of the country, but Estonian almost everywhere else.

Left: **A brief meeting on the streets of Tallinn.**

Opposite: **Unlike Slavic languages, such as Russian, Estonian uses the Roman alphabet.**

Advertisements for computers in Estonian.

ESTONIAN

Estonian is the native language of perhaps as many as one million people in Estonia today and is spoken to varying degrees of fluency by people of Estonian descent in Sweden, Germany, the United States, Canada, and Britain. Estonian belongs to the Finno-Ugric family of languages, spoken only by Magyars (Hungarians), Finns, and Estonians. It is most closely related to Finnish, and Estonians and Finns have little trouble understanding each other.

A considerable amount of German vocabulary has become part of the Estonian language over the years. However, much of the German influence was "Estonianized" when the country became independent in 1919.

Johannes Aavik (1880–1973) is credited with having introduced some important linguistic innovations, including expanding Estonian vocabulary to include a number of Finnish words that offer greater flexibility. Finnish loan words have easily been incorporated into the language. In recent years, many English words have also become common.

Unlike Slavic languages, such as Russian, Estonian uses the Roman alphabet. Early written Estonian was strongly Germanic in character. The first text to appear in the Estonian language

Customers sift through second-hand books at a book fair.

was a translation of the Lutheran catechism in 1535. A New Testament in the southern Estonian dialect did not appear until 1680, and a northern version in 1715. Using the northern dialect as a basis, Anton Thor Helle united the two dialects and translated a full Bible (1739). Käsu Hans wrote the first known example of secular literature in a poem where he laments the destruction of Tartu in the Great Northern War. The language began to develop fully with the flowering of an Estonian literary movement in the 19th century, including the appearance of the first native Estonian poet, Kristjan Jaak Peterson. Freidrich Kreutzwald's epic compilation, the *Kalevipoeg*, established an authentic Estonian literary tradition, of which the poet Lydia Koidula was one of the greatest examples.

Estonian is considered a difficult language to master. There are 14 different cases for each noun, while grammatical categories are usually marked by suffixes added to the stem of the noun or verb. Like English, Estonian is an idiomatic language. There are no articles or genders in Estonian. For a country whose national identity is so closely associated with the land, it is not surprising to find Estonian names such as Ilves (lynx), Maasikas (strawberry), and Rohumaa (grassland).

The Baltic countries hosted their first International Book Fair in Tallinn in 1995, attracting visitors and exhibitors from many countries, most of whom represented English-language publishers.

ESTONIAN DIALECTS Estonian has two major dialects—a Tallinn-based, northern dialect, and a more rural southern dialect. Recently, linguists have further divided Estonian into eight subdialects, including northeastern coastal, central, insular (island), eastern, and western, plus three main dialects of the south: Mulgi, Tartu, and Võru.

ESTONIAN SWEDISH Estonian Swedish belongs to the eastern group of dialects of the Swedish language. Isolated from the mother tongue, Estonian Swedish has many archaic characteristics and is not easily understood by modern Swedes. There are only about 100 people in Estonia who can speak Estonian Swedish. Ordinary Swedish is popular for cultural and business reasons.

OTHER LANGUAGES

English, German, and French are becoming increasingly popular. English and German are widely spoken in the tourist areas of Tallinn and Tartu. English is fast becoming a lingua franca among young people.

FINNISH Finnish is spoken in much of northern Estonia: it is estimated that at least 5,000 people speak it as their mother tongue, while many more speak it as a second language. Because of its similarity to Estonian, Tallinners in particular speak some Finnish because of the regular inflow of Finnish tourists and business people from Helsinki.

RUSSIAN Russian is a familiar language in Estonia. Until independence, many Estonians were required to speak Russian in order to communicate with the authorities. Consequently, many Estonians are fluent in Russian, even if they rarely speak it.

PRONUNCIATION

Estonian is considered one of the most beautiful languages in the world, perhaps because of its numerous long vowels and few harsh consonants.

a	"u" as in "but"	s	like the English "s", but voiceless and weaker
b	voiceless, like the "p" in "copy"		
(c)		š	"sh" as in "shoe"—appears only in foreign words
d	voiceless, like the "t" in "city"		
e	"e" as in "bet"	z	"s" as in "is"
(f)		ž	"s" as in "pleasure"—used only in foreign words
g	voiceless, like the "ck" in "ticket"		
h	"h" as in "house"	t	"t" as in "tall"
i	"i" as in "pin"	u	"u" as in "put"
j	"y" as in "yes"	v	"v" as in "violet"
k	"k" as in "kitchen"	(w)	
l	"l" as in "lily"	õ	"ir" as in "girl"
m	"m" as in "mother"	ä	"a" as in "cat"
n	"n" as in "not"	ö	"u" as in "fur" (but with rounded lips)
o	"o" as in "off"		
p	"p" as in "pot"	ü	"oo" as in "boot"
(q)		(x)	
r	the "r" is usually rolled	(y)	

In Estonian, double vowels elongate the regular vowel sound. Estonian is also famous for its unusual contrast of three degrees of consonant and vowel length. For example, *koli* ("KO-li," junk) is pronounced with a short "o" sound, while *kooli* ("KOH-li," of school) uses a longer "o," and *kooli* ("KOO-li," to school) has an extra long "o."

aa	"a" as in "father"
ee	"eh" as in the interjection "eh?"
ii	"ee" as in "feel"
oo	"eau" as in "bureau"
uu	"oo" as in "food"
ää	same as "ä" but with a more open mouth
öö	same as "ö," but longer and higher
õõ	same as "õ," but longer
üü	same as "ü," but longer and clearer

A newsstand displaying the various newspapers available. A few English-language newspapers are published in Estonia, including *The Baltic Times* and Tallinn's leading English-language newspaper, *The City Paper*, which offers helpful information to visitors.

NEWSPAPERS AND PUBLICATIONS

In the 1970s and 1980s, there were about 50 officially recognized newspapers. Between 1988 and 1990, about 400 new magazines and newspapers appeared. Most of these new publications were politically radical and were a natural expression of the fundamental changes that were occurring in the Soviet Union.

Since independence, the rising cost of newsprint and postage has reduced the number of newspapers. Seventy percent are published in Estonian. The main national Estonian-language newspapers include *Hommikuleht* (Morning Paper), *Eesti Ekspress* (Estonian Express), *Eesti Päevaleht* (Estonian Daily), and *Postimees* (The Postman), which is Estonia's oldest newspaper and has been published in Tartu since 1855. Although the constitution provides for freedom of the press, high-quality investigative journalism is only just beginning to appear, following decades when the press was merely a government mouthpiece. Foreign newspapers and magazines are also widely available.

TELEVISION

Television broadcasting has been slowly improving since independence, especially with the appearance of independent operators and foreign programming. There are several major independent television channels, as well as the state-run Estonian Television. The latter broadcasts programs in both Estonian and Russian and has a reputation for being dull and unimaginative. State-run broadcast media continue to receive government subsidies. Tallinn Commercial Television operates one channel that broadcasts in Estonian and Russian. Other commercial channels include Kanal 2, which broadcasts classic Estonian and Hollywood movies, and Tipp TV, which offers American programming with Estonian subtitles. There are also a number of regional television channels.

For many years people living in the north of the country have been able to watch Finnish television—in Tallinn as many as four Finnish stations are available. In the Soviet era, Finnish television offered Estonians a window on the Western world and a glimpse of another lifestyle.

A family shops for a new television set. Since independence, the quality of programming has increased dramatically.

ARTS

UNTIL THE 19TH CENTURY, traditional Estonian culture existed mainly in the form of peasant folktales and verses, passed down through the ages by word of mouth. Estonian folk poetry proved a resilient and important force in maintaining Estonian identity, helping Estonians retain a sense of their culture despite many centuries of foreign occupation. Estonia's national awakening in the late 19th century was centered around a development and exploration of the country's folklore and folk traditions, providing the basis for a separate Estonian culture and thriving literary, musical, and artistic movements.

Since independence, Estonia's artistic heritage has played an important part in rebuilding people's sense of national identity. The Estonian Heritage Society was created in 1987 with the mandate of preserving and promoting the artistic and historical culture of Estonia, and to date, it has been very successful.

Left: **Folk dancers perform outside Tallinn's city wall.**

Opposite: **A woman sells her paintings at an art fair.**

Playing the fiddle and accordion outside a traditional restaurant.

MUSIC AND SINGING

Music and singing are Estonia's most important and popular forms of artistic expression. Folk singing originated in Estonia in the first millennium B.C. as runic verse—short tunes with a limited range, but rich in variation. These songs were accompanied by traditional instruments, such as the *kannel* ("KUHN-ehl," a kind of zither), whistles, pipes, flutes, and fiddles. Rhyming folk songs did not appear until the 18th century.

Estonia's first symphony orchestra was founded in 1900 in Tartu. Rudolph Tobias wrote the first Estonian symphonic work, the prelude *Julius Caesar*, in 1896 and followed this with a piano concerto (1897) and oratorio (1909). Estonian symphonic music reached fruition in the country's first period of independence between 1920 and 1940. Estonia's first significant opera, *The Vikings*, was written by Evald Aav. Eduard Tubin wrote the first Estonian ballet, *The Goblin*, in 1943. He fled to Sweden at the end of World War II to escape persecution under the Soviet occupation.

Most recently, Veljo Tormis has revived ancient forms of runic chanting and uses them in his choral works. His best-known works, which are notoriously difficult to perform, are *Curse Upon Iron* and *The Ingrian Evenings*, both part of a cycle of songs. Currently, Arvo Pärt is Estonia's most widely acclaimed international composer, famous for his minimalist style and choral compositions. His best-known choral works are *Tabula Rasa, St. John's Passion, Cantus*, and *Fratres*.

From October to April, classical performances are held almost every night at Tallinn's Estonian Concert Hall. Performances are given by the Symphony Orchestra of the Tallinn Conservatoire, or by the Philharmonic Chamber Orchestra and Choir. The latter is the best-known Estonian choir of the 1990s. Their recording of Pärt's *Te Deum* was nominated for a Grammy award. Small ensembles and solo performers also play in smaller halls and theaters in Tallinn, Tartu, and Pärnu. Tallinn's Estonian Theater stages musicals, ballets, and operas.

Popular music, probably Estonia's most rapidly expanding art form, plays a major role in Estonia's celebrated summer music festivals. Both foreign and local rock, rhythm and blues, soul, and jazz bands have a wide following. Popular 1990s bands include Compromise Blue, Thieving Nightingale, Clementine, Mr. Lawrence, and the folk rockers Jääboiler. The rock singer Alo Mattiisen is popular for using Estonian folk chants in some of his songs. Rock music is still associated with the "singing revolution" of the late 1980s, a gesture of defiance the Estonian people will remember proudly for generations.

Arvo Pärt was among a group of modernist experimenters who were denounced by the Soviet authorities in the 1960s.

LITERATURE

A wealth of Estonian folk poetry from ancient times has been kept alive through the centuries in an oral tradition. These stories—passed down from generation to generation—provided the fledgling Estonian literary movement with material and a sense of tradition. Today, there are more than a billion pages of folk poetry preserved in the national archives in Tartu.

Because Estonia experienced a long period of foreign domination, an Estonian-language literature developed quite late—only in the middle of the 19th century, at the time of Estonia's national awakening. Kristjan Jaak Peterson (1801–22) is considered Estonia's first real poet. The two men who are considered to have done the most to develop Estonian literature —Freidrich Faehlmann (1798–1850) and Freidrich Kreutzwald (1803–82)—were both doctors with a close interest in Estonian folklore. Faehlmann collected verses of folk poetry from rural Estonia. After his untimely death, Kreutzwald continued his work. Between 1857 and 1861 Kreutzwald compiled Estonia's national epic, the *Kalevipoeg* (Son of Kalev). The epic consists of 19,023 runic verses and tells the story of the son of Kalev, the mythical father of the Estonian nation.

Perno Postimees, Estonia's first Estonian-language newspaper, was first published in 1857 by Johann Jannsen (1819–1890). It contributed significantly to the national awakening. Jannsen's daughter, Lydia, who wrote under the pen name Lydia Koidula (1843–86), produced some highly emotive and patriotic poetry. Many consider her collection of verse, *The Nightingale of Emajogi*, to be the most important literary work from Estonia's period of national awakening.

Toward the end of the 19th century, writing novels became more popular. Eduard Bornhöhe (1862–1923) wrote romantic novels. *The Avenger*, written in 1880, revives Estonia's troubled past by depicting the struggle against the German Crusaders. The most prominent writer in the realism genre was Eduard Vilde (1865–1933). His novel, *Banished*, written in 1896, is a stylistic landmark in Estonian fiction. In the historical trilogy, *The Dairyman of Mäeküla* (1916), Vilde portrayed the inequalities of the Baltic-German feudal system. He also wrote plays, including *The Untamed*

Miracle (1912) and *The Fire Dragon* (1913). His contemporary, the poet and story writer Juhan Liiv's (1864–1913) most notable works are *Ten Stories* (1893), *The Shed* (1894), and *Poems* (1909).

A group calling themselves *Noor Eesti* (Young Estonia) sought to free the Estonian language from its parochialisms and laid the foundation of modern Estonian literature. Chief among them were Gustav Suits (1883–1956), Friedebert Tuglas (1886–1971), and Johannes Aavik (1880–1973). During the independence era, *Siuru*, a literary group that took its name from a mythical songbird, shocked conventional taste by exploring sensual and erotic themes. Marie Under (1883–1980) was by far the most gifted member of this group, bursting on the scene with evocative, exciting, and emotional poetry of a power not previously experienced in Estonia. This period also produced Anton Hansen Tammsaare (1878–1940), considered to be Estonia's greatest novelist. His most impressive work, the five-volume *Truth and Justice* (1926–33), explores Estonian social and political life from the 1870s to the 1920s.

Jaan Kross is probably Estonia's most famous contemporary writer, and many of his works have been translated into English. Kross is best known

Jaan Kross, the distinguished Estonian writer who won the 1988 Soviet Trades Union Prize for his novel *The Czar's Madman*.

for *The Czar's Madman* (1978), a novel where he tackled contemporary Soviet issues through a historical theme. Jaan Kaplinski and Paul-Eerik Rummo are Estonia's best-known modern poets. Both Kross and Kaplinski were elected to the *Riikikogu* in 1992, while Rummo was made minister of culture the same year.

THEATER

Theater is extremely popular in Estonia, and there are major theaters in Tallinn, Pärnu, Rakvere, Tartu, and Viljandi. Ten theaters are maintained by local governments. The oldest theater in Estonia is the Vanemuine, which was built in Tartu in 1870. Estonian drama was born of the same seeds as Estonian literature, springing from the period of national awakening at the end of the 19th century. Lydia Koidula's *The Cousin from Saaremaa* (1870) was the first Estonian play to be staged.

In the Soviet era, the theater, along with other institutions, was used by the communist authorities for propaganda purposes and was heavily censored. Mainly Russian plays were performed. The "thaw" following Stalin's death allowed the innovative theater enthusiast Voldemar Panso to found a drama school at the Tallinn Conservatoire in 1957. In 1965 he also founded the popular Youth Theater. Popular avant-garde theater was introduced in the 1960s by Evald Hermaküla and Jaan Tooming.

Today the most popular theater in the country is the Estonian Drama Theater in Tallinn, which developed in the 1950s. Many classic Western plays are popular and are interpreted in an Estonian style. Plays are almost always performed in Estonian, except those of the Russian Drama Theater in Tallinn, which performs many classic 19th and 20th century Russian plays. Well-known actors include Ita Ever, Tiia Kriisa, Aarne Üksküla, Andrus Vaarik, and Tõnu Kark.

MOVIES

From the beginning of the Soviet occupation until the political thaw following Stalin's death, Estonian film-making consisted of documentaries and newsreels, mostly of a crudely political style. Movies with artistic merit did not begin to appear until the 1960s. Kaljo Kiisk's *Lunacy* (1968) was the first, and tackled social issues. Leida Laius' *Smile, Please* (1985) and *A Stolen Meeting* (1988) also received international recognition. Peeter Simm has directed historical movies, including *Ideal Landscape* (1980) and *The Man Who Never Was* (1989).

Above all else, Estonia has become famous for producing puppet and animated movies. Puppet movie-making began in 1957 with Elbert Tuganov, who directed *Bloody John* (1974). Rein Raamat has achieved international success for his animated movies *The Flight* (1973), *Tõll the Great* (1980), and *The Hell* (1983). Priit Pärn has also received worldwide recognition for *The Triangle* (1982), *Time Out* (1984), *Breakfast on the Grass* (1987), *The Turtle's End-Game* (1990), and *Hotel E* (1991).

VISUAL ARTS

Estonia's first art school was opened at Tartu University in 1803 but Estonian national art did not really take off until the period of national awakening. In 1906 the first general exhibition of Estonian art was held in Tartu.

Following Estonia's first period of independence, Estonian art split into a plethora of schools, including cubism, abstract expressionism, and neo-impressionism. During World War II and the Soviet occupation many Estonian artists fled to the West. In the 1960s, following Stalin's death, art again began to develop. By the 1970s, there was a profusion of artists and a thriving art scene in Estonia. Despite Soviet attempts to force Estonian art into the straitjacket of social realism, Estonian artists maintained their connection with European traditions.

Painting in the park.

ARCHITECTURE

Estonia's architectural heritage is dominated by the Gothic style of the Germans and Swedes, who ruled the country from the 13th to the 18th century. Many castles and fortifications were also built by the Germans and Swedes.

Tallinn is one of the most architecturally impressive cities in the Baltic region and has some well-preserved medieval buildings in a predominantly German style. The city walls date from the 14th–16th centuries. Most of the guild halls, churches, and residences in the Old Town and Toompea also date from this period. The best example of Renaissance architecture is the Blackhead's Fraternity Building (built 1597) in Tallinn, complete with intricately carved facade and portico. The Baroque style of architecture, dating from the 17th and 18th centuries, can be seen in Narva's restored Town Hall (originally built in 1671). Tsarist Russian rule brought a more classical style of architecture to Estonia. Many of the manor houses that have survived in Estonia were built in this period, as were the main buildings of Tartu University and Tartu Town Hall. Nineteenth century architecture was dominated by Baltic-German architects trained in Riga and St. Petersburg.

By the 1920s, architects were for the first time educated in Tallinn. The Art Nouveau style became popular, exemplified by the Parliament Building in Tallinn (built 1922). A more functional style dominated in the 1930s. Examples of this style are the Tallinn Art House and the Pärnu Beach Hotel. In the Soviet period, emphasis was placed on cheap, practical, industrial housing. Many of these prefab monstrosities can be seen on the edges of towns and cities, especially in the northeast and around Tallinn.

Estonia has some simple but impressive early churches, including the 13th century Karja Church on Saaremaa Island and the ruined Jaani Church in Tartu. The Karja Church has many marvellous sculptures of 13th century village life.

The well-preserved Narva Town Hall.

LEISURE

ESTONIAN'S LEISURE ACTIVITIES ARE limited by both the country's geography and climate. In the winter, indoor activities, such as watching television, reading, and playing chess, are all popular. Estonians are generally well-read, and their interest in chess has in the past gained the country some recognition internationally through the success of Paul Keres. In the summer, people like to go to the country or the coast and enjoy the outdoors while the weather is warm.

Estonians' love of singing and music is demonstrated by the country's hugely popular song and music festivals. Choral societies and choirs exist in every part of the country. In urban areas, jazz and rock bars are popular. In Tallinn, Tartu, and Pärnu, bars and clubs are packed every Friday and Saturday night with people enjoying local rhythm and blues, rock, and jazz. Pärnu in particular is filled with music in the summer because of the influx of tourists and music events hosted by resorts. Young people also go to clubs and discos in the larger cities. Classical, opera, and choral works are well attended: concerts are held at the Estonian Concert Hall in Tallinn three times a week.

As in most countries, people like to watch movies. Increasingly, American and European movies and documentaries are being shown with Estonian subtitles.

RURAL PURSUITS

In Estonia, attachment to the land is strong. In the summer, favorite pastimes are walking and picking berries and mushrooms in the woods and forests. Camping on the coast, in the parks, or in the countryside is popular. Estonia has many campsites in the quiet rural areas. Estonia's lakes are sites for relaxation, and swimming is popular in the summer. Some lakes, such as Lake Püha near Otepää, also have beaches. Lake Püha has a captivating, mystical atmosphere and was blessed by the Dalai Lama when he visited Tartu in 1992. Fishing is also a popular summer pursuit. In the winter, people fish by smashing the ice on the lakes.

Winter pastimes include skiing, ice-skating, and tobogganing. Estonia's flat landscape and extensive winter snowfall make cross-country skiing a popular pursuit as well. The Otepää highlands receive more snow than any other part of the country. The town of Otepää is Estonia's winter sports center—there is downhill skiing, ski jumping, and numerous cross-country routes for enthusiasts. Each February 12,000 Estonians and foreigners brave the freezing weather to participate in the Tartu Ski Marathon.

Fishing on the river at Tartu.

VACATIONS

Most urban Estonians take their summer vacation in the country, usually going to the national parks, islands, or picturesque regions in the south. The woods, islands, and lakes still offer a pristine freshness not found in many other parts of Europe. The low population density and undeveloped infrastructure mean buildings and fences rarely block a path or view, giving the land an inviting openness. Pärnu is the most popular city destination.

Following the economic success of the 1990s, more Estonians are taking vacations abroad. Finland and Sweden are by far the most popular foreign destinations, and quickly and easily reached by passenger ferry from Tallinn. Estonians also travel overland to Russia, Lithuania, Germany, Norway, and Latvia—some go as far afield as France, Spain, Italy, Britain, and Holland. Flying is still a luxury for Estonians, and few people travel as far as North America.

RESORTS AND SPAS

Estonia is blessed with many health resorts, ranging from coastal beaches to sanatoriums, spa towns, lakeside camps, and curative mud baths. The sanatorium in Kuressaare on Saaremaa Island has specialized in baths of curative sea mud since 1876. The mud gives off a terrible smell, and only the most dedicated mud bathers endure the treatment.

Pärnu is famous for its promenade and beaches. The Baltic Sea's shallow waters make bathing both warm and safe in the summer months. In the winter, the water is ice-cold and few people dare to swim.

Haapsalu was developed as a spa town in the 19th century, though its curative mud is now considered of poor quality. A railroad was built to provide access to the town for the Russian aristocracy, and a long, covered platform shelters visitors from the rain. Tchaikovsky, the famous Russian composer, often visited Haapsalu in the summer, where he is said to have borrowed a motif from an Estonian folk song when composing his 6th Symphony. Haapsalu's Paralepa forested park and beach are popular with vacationers.

NATURE'S DOCTOR

Saunas are a fundamental aspect of Estonian rural life and a pastime Estonia has in common with Scandinavian countries. In the past, peasants took saunas to treat illnesses rather than incur the expense of calling a doctor. A basic sauna consists of a wooden room with benches and a hot stove, usually surrounded by bricks or stones, on which you toss water to produce clouds of steam. The steam helps open the bathers' pores and provides relaxation and a welcome relief from the extreme cold in the winter. Saunas are said to be good for the lungs. Bathers often lightly brush their bodies with bunches of birch twigs, an action that increases perspiration and tingles the nerve ends. Taking a sauna is considered a highly personal experience, and an invitation to share a sauna is a friendly and hospitable gesture.

SPORTS

Estonia has been internationally successful in many sports, especially wrestling. It is commonly remarked that sport in Estonia began with Georg Lürich, who won the Greco-Roman world wrestling championship in 1901. Lürich, a remarkable athlete, was also a champion weightlifter. The first Estonian to win an Olympic medal was the wrestler Martin Klein, in 1912. In 1923 the Estonian Olympic Committee was created in the newly independent country, and Estonia achieved international success in track and field events. Estonia's international marksmen team won competitions in the 1920s and 1930s, and won the *Copa Argentina* three times (1935, 1937, and 1939).

From 1945 until 1991, Estonian sportsmen and women represented the USSR in sporting competitions. Jaan Talts, a champion weightlifter, was three times world champion and four times European champion in the 1960s and 1970s. Heino Lipp was decathlon champion in the postwar years, though the Soviet authorities never allowed him to compete in the

To honor his accomplishments, Paul Keres's portrait appears on the Estonian five-kroon note.

Olympic Games because of his public disavowal of communism. However, Lipp attended the 1992 Olympic Games and carried the Estonian flag in Estonia's first Olympic competition after the breakup of the USSR.

In 1989 Estonian sports were reorganized and the national Olympic committee restored. From 1920 to 1993, Estonians won more than 300 gold medals in Olympic, European, and World championships—an impressive tally for one of Europe's smallest nations.

Estonians have also achieved success in sailing. All the sailing events at the 1980 Moscow Olympics were held in Tallinn, leaving Estonia with first-class sailing facilities.

In cycling, Aavo Pikkuus won the Soviet road racing championship in 1975 and 1976, while Erika Salumäe—Estonia's most accomplished female cyclist—won an Olympic gold medal as part of the Soviet sprinting team in 1988. Four years later she won another gold medal at the Barcelona Olympics, competing this time under the Estonian flag.

The former USSR was renowned for producing top chess players. Emerging in the 1930s, Estonian Paul Keres was one of the best chess players in the world for 40 years. Three times Soviet chess champion, Keres played in 66 international tournaments, winning seven Olympic gold medals.

Basketball is the most popular sport in Estonia today. It grew in popularity during the Soviet period. Today, Tallinn's basketball teams, which include Baltika Tallinn, BC Tallinn, and BC Kalev Tallinn, are among the best in Europe. Ice hockey and soccer are also popular sports.

SAILING

In a country with a long coastline and numerous islands, sailing is a natural pastime. The Baltic Sea is very shallow and freezes easily, consequently sailing is a summer activity. Estonia's waters are considered the best in the region for sailing, and the Pirita Olympic Sports Center is one of the best equipped. The center was originally built for the 1980 Olympic Games. Haapsalu is one of the few other places in Estonia to have a yacht club, opened in 1992. It successfully hosted the World Ice Yachting Championship in 1991. There are few other proper marinas in Estonia, and yachts, dinghies, and sailboats bob on the waters of fishing ports throughout the country.

A marina on Pirita River. Sailing on the rivers is safer than sailing in the strait between the west coast and the islands of Hiiumaa, Vormsi, and Muhu. The Muhu channel is marked throughout with buoys, and only the most skillful sailors navigate it without problems.

FESTIVALS

ESTONIA IS HOME TO many festivals and cultural events, especially during the summer months. Tallinn in particular comes alive from May to September. Many regions and towns have their own local celebrations when people dress in traditional clothes. On festival days it is traditional to brew and drink beer, a custom Estonians have had no problem maintaining over the centuries.

Song festivals have long held political significance in Estonia. The first song festival was in 1869 during the country's national and cultural reawakening. Under Soviet rule, the song festivals became one of the few legal means for Estonians to celebrate their identity and express national pride. It was at the *Baltika* folk festival in 1987 that the national flags of the former Baltic republics were first publicly displayed without the offenders being arrested. These displays of nationalism were the beginning of the movement later dubbed the "Singing Revolution."

Left: **Three hundred thousand people gathered for the 1988 "Singing Revolution."**

Opposite: **The opening ceremony of the Tallinn Song Festival.**

MUSIC FESTIVALS

Throughout the Baltic countries song and dance festivals are held every summer. These events attract many visitors, especially Baltic people living abroad. The amphitheater of Tallinn's song festival grounds can hold up to 30,000 singers and has space for an audience of more than 150,000. Such is the popularity of singing festivals that there is rarely an empty seat.

The National Song Festival takes place every five years, in late June or early July. This weekend event is the country's oldest song festival. Five hundred thousand people attended the 1990 Song Festival, almost half the ethnic Estonian population. It was an extremely emotional event that climaxed with a mass choir of 30,000 singers singing Estonian national songs.

Rock Summer is the Baltic's biggest rock music festival. For three days in July, well-known international and local acts play to a packed stadium. Rock Summer is gaining international recognition and has been broadcast on British television and MTV Europe.

FiESTa music festival is a week-long extravaganza of live jazz, blues, new age, and world music. It is celebrated yearly in Pärnu in the second half of June. In recent years FiESTa has also been accompanied by the Baltoscandal drama festival. Together, the two festivals bring around 40 musical acts and 20 theater groups to Pärnu, filling the bars, restaurants, and streets. Pärnu also hosts a 10-day classical music festival in early July.

Smaller, local song festivals are held throughout the country. Since 1984 Estonia has hosted an International Organ Music Festival, usually held in early August, when some of the world's leading organists perform in Tallinn's beautiful, historic churches. The festival often moves around the country, playing in various locations.

National dress in the brightest colors at a choral concert.

FOLK FESTIVALS

By far the most important folk festival in the Baltic is the *Baltika* folk festival, held annually in one of the three Baltic countries each summer. The festival celebrates the folklore and culture of small, little-known ethnic groups from throughout Europe. Folk dancers and singers from Estonia, Lithuania, and Latvia gather to celebrate the week-long festival with dancing, singing, parades, and exhibitions.

There are numerous other folk festivals. Every June, Old Tallinn Days celebrates traditional Estonian culture with much jollity, music, and dancing through the streets of the capital's Old Town. In early September, Tallinn also hosts *Lillepidu*, an international flower festival that attracts thousands of spectators.

MIDSUMMER

The holidays of *Võidupüha* ("VO-it-u-pih-hah"—
Victory Day) and *Jaanipäev* ("JAH-ni-pa-ehv—
St. John's Day") on June 23 and 24 combine the
age-old pagan festival of Midsummer with the
more modern, nationalistic celebration of the
Battle of Võnnu, where, in 1919, the Estonian
army thwarted the Baltic German army's attempt
to regain control of Estonia.

As can be expected from a region where
summers are short and winters are long, dark,
and cold, Midsummer night has been a major
celebration since pagan times and is deeply
rooted in Estonian peasant culture. *Jaanipäev*
marks the longest day of the year when the
evening twilight and emerging dawn seem to
become one. At this time of year the light never
fully fades. On the night of June 23 and morning
of June 24, villagers gather around a bonfire to
sing, dance, and make merry.

In the past, Midsummer night was considered
a time of sorcery and magic. Purifying bonfires
were lit to fend off evil spirits. Traditionally,
people would also leap over the bonfires—
superstition has it that a successful clearance
indicates a successful year ahead. *Võidupüha*
and *Jaanipäev* usually merge into one long
holiday.

THE SINGING TREE

Folk instruments, along with folk dress, are featured in Estonian festivals. In Estonia most traditional instruments are those that are common throughout northern and eastern Europe: the zither, whistle, accordion, flute, goathorn, and violin. The guitar is also widely played. The one instrument unique to the Baltic lands is the *kannel*.

The *kannel* is a kind of zither that has between 5 and 12 iron or natural fiber strings pulled taut over a board. This instrument has been used in the region for at least 3,000 years. The name derives from a proto-Baltic word meaning "the singing tree." The *kannel* is considered sacred, and according to folklore, the tree from which the instrument is to be made must be cut when someone has died but is not yet buried. The fine, deeply affecting

tones of the instrument have come to symbolize Estonia's traditional national music. In the Soviet period, a many-stringed version of the instrument was developed to play Soviet-approved folk music.

Since the 1980s renewed interest in traditional music has led to a revival of the original *kannel*, plus an interest in other traditional instruments like the Jew's harp, bagpipe, reed, whistle, clappers, and rattles. Many of the simpler traditional instruments are made by the players themselves, while the more sophisticated instruments, such as the bagpipes or *kannel*, are made by a few trained masters.

INDEPENDENCE DAY

Estonians celebrate their independence on February 24, the day the Republic of Estonia was first declared in 1918. The declaration was followed by a two-year war of independence, where the fledgling Estonian army held off attacks by the Russian Red army and the Baltic German forces. The Tartu Peace Treaty of 1920 secured Estonia's borders for the first time in the country's history. Estonians take great pride in marking their hard-won independence, which serves as a permanent reminder of the Soviet Union's illegal 50-year occupation. People celebrate by gathering to eat and drink, while the Estonian flag hangs from almost every building as an expression of national pride. The day is officially marked with the raising of the Estonian national flag at dawn from an old tower in Tallinn.

RELIGIOUS HOLIDAYS

The vast majority of ethnic Estonians are nominally Lutheran in faith. Although they celebrate the major festivals of Christmas and Easter, the Christian holidays do not create the kind of excitement or activity associated with the song festivals.

Christmas is celebrated in much the same way as in other northern European countries. Most Estonians celebrate by having a meal, visiting family and friends, and relaxing in their homes. Often the close proximity of the New Year provides them with an excuse to have a long midwinter break. Shrove Tuesday—during the seventh week before Easter—is usually observed in February. Children often go tobogganing on this day; it is believed that a long sleigh slide indicates a fruitful summer harvest. At Easter time, people dye eggs and give eggs as presents. Traditionally, eggs were dyed using onion skins or leaves from birch switches. Shops, offices, and businesses are usually closed from the Thursday before Good Friday until the Tuesday after Easter Monday.

A family gathering on Christmas Day.

FOOD

ESTONIAN COOKING IS WHOLESOME fare based on a traditional, rural diet with few frills and no spices. The main ingredients of the Estonian diet are meat (especially pork), bread, fruit, root vegetables, and varieties of mushrooms, berries, and nuts in the summer. Fresh milk is also a dominant ingredient, as is cheese, especially for making sauces. Estonians tend to bake, roast, or boil their food: very little traditional Baltic food is fried.

A typical breakfast in Estonia might include any or all of the following: porridge, cottage cheese, bread with salted fish, and fried eggs with smoked ham, all washed down with plenty of coffee or sometimes tea. Dinner is likely to consist of three courses: a substantial first course of cold dishes followed by roast pork with potatoes and other vegetables and finished off with a mousse, sweet bread soup, or baked apples, depending on the season. Traditionally, supper is a lighter meal than dinner, consisting of roast meats or pickled fish. It is the custom for people to say *"Head isu!"* ("HEH-uht i-su"), which roughly translates as "Bon appétit," before commencing a meal.

BREAD

Leib ("LEH-ip"), or bread, is the essential staple of the Estonian diet and accompanies every meal. Because of food shortages in the past bread has attained an almost religious significance among Estonians. Consequently, bread is never thrown away but often reappears in a different guise, such as in *leiva supp* ("LEH-iv-uh soop"), a sweet, black, bread soup.

Most Estonian bread is of the dark brown, wholemeal variety. Bread made from barley is a speciality and is often sweetened with honey. Rye bread (*Rukkileib*—"RUK-ki-leh-ip") enhanced with molasses is also popular and a perfect accompaniment for Estonia's mild cheeses and spicy beer.

Traditionally, bread made from refined white flour is eaten only on special occasions. The ultimate white bread is kringel *("KRIN-kehl"), a large, braided loaf filled with nuts and raisins and prepared in the shape of a pretzel.* Kringel *is usually served on birthdays and holidays.*

Opposite: **Buying fruit at the village market.**

ROSOLJE

3 teaspoons dried mustard powder
$1/2$ teaspoon sugar
$1/2$ pint (300 ml) whipping cream
5 large, boiled beetroots, peeled and diced
2 apples, cored, peeled, and diced
6 large potatoes, boiled, peeled and diced
2 gherkins, diced

2 fillets of pickled herring, drained
   and diced
1 pound (450 g) lean cooked beef or pork,
   trimmed and diced
2 tablespoons (30 ml) dry white wine
salt and freshly ground black pepper
2 hardboiled eggs, chopped

Combine mustard, sugar, and whipping cream in a small bowl. Whip the mustard cream until it starts to show soft peaks. Set aside.

In a separate bowl, combine vegetables, herring, meat, wine, salt, and pepper.

Add eggs and three-quarters of the mustard cream and mix together. Chill for 30 minutes, then transfer to a lettuce-lined plate or bowl and top with the remaining mustard cream.

THE COLD TABLE

Cured meats, such as goose and ham, are popular traditional dishes in the eastern Baltic, dating from a time when the lack of refrigeration made preserving meat a necessity.

The first course in most Estonian meals is a selection of cold dishes. Traditionally, two-thirds of the meal consisted of cold dishes; as in Sweden and Russia, it is still considered the best way of showing off local produce. Often, these cold dishes are as substantial as the main course. *Rosolje* ("roh-SOHL-juh"), a delicious salad based on beetroot, meat, and herring, is the signature dish of Estonian cuisine. It is often served as a first course or as a luncheon dish on a warm summer day. Small pies called *pirukas* ("PI-ru-kuhs"), filled with meat, carrots, and cabbage, are also served.

Fish is a part of the cold table. Herring is popular throughout the Baltic, pickled or mixed with seasonings such as mustard, onions, or sour cream.

MEAT AND POTATOES

Estonian food is very much of the "meat and potatoes" variety, covered in a rich gravy. Potatoes were introduced by the Baltic Germans in the 18th century and have been a mainstay of the Estonian diet ever since. Pork is the most important meat and is eaten in various forms: roasted, cured, bacon, ham, or in pies, sausage, and black (blood sausage) pudding. Sauerkraut (cabbage fermented in brine) is often served with pork.

SOUPS AND DESSERTS

Estonia's soups are generally bland, creamy dishes made chiefly from milk and vegetables, or perhaps with yogurt and dill cucumber. Unusually, many soups are eaten as desserts. *Kissell* ("KI-sehl"), a clear, sweet soup, is made from garden berries and red currants and served with white bread. Raspberry soup—liquidized raspberries boiled and whisked into a soup, then served with a dash of lemon and sour cream—is delicious, and restaurants in Tallinn consider it their speciality. Desserts including berries, apples, and rhubarb appear in various guises—whether stewed or baked in a pie—characteristic of a traditional rural diet. Baked apple, for example, is usually served with milk and sugar. *Torte* ("TORH-teh"), a favorite party dessert, came to Estonia as a legacy of the Baltic barons. Fluffy, plate-size pancakes, usually filled with raspberries or blueberries, are also popular. Sweet whipped cream is often added to cakes and pies.

Garden produce plays a vital part in Estonian cuisine. In rural areas, people grow tomatoes, peas, cucumbers, beetroots, swedes, courgettes, turnips, potatoes, cabbages, and rhubarb. Apple and plum trees are also numerous. From beyond the garden, wild nuts, berries, and mushrooms have been gathered for centuries from the surrounding woods and fields.

A summer feast with friends and family.

Bottling homemade wine on a farm in southern Estonia.

THIRST QUENCHERS

Traditional drinks include ales and meads, teas brewed from plants found in the garden or woods, and milk. Juices, or cordials, made from local summer fruit such as gooseberries, rhubarb, and juniper have been enjoyed in the region for centuries. A liking for coffee rather than tea distinguishes the Baltic peoples from their Slavic neighbors, and coffee houses and cafés are numerous throughout Estonia's cities and towns.

Lager and ale of the dark variety found in other parts of northern Europe have traditionally been brewed in Estonia. Saare beer, brewed on the island of Saaremaa, is considered one of Estonia's best traditional beers, while Saku Reval Luksus is a popular, Western-style, bottled beer. Kvass is a rye-based beer of Russian origin.

Popular spirits include cognac, vodka, and the locally produced Vana Tallinn liqueur. For many years, people in the Baltic countries have made their own moonshine vodka from rye, or perhaps sugar and water and a few peas.

EATING OUT

Since independence, the choice of both Estonian and international cuisines available in Estonia's towns and cities has dramatically improved. Tallinn in particular offers Chinese, Korean, Italian, Middle Eastern, and Indian food, as well as many restaurants serving hearty, traditional Estonian cuisine. Local fast-food chains offering pizza, pasta, salads, and burgers, as well as the better-known international burger chains, can be found in every part of the country. After work, Estonia's cafés are swamped by people seeking good coffee and tasty pastries. Tallinn's many dark, stuffy cellar bars are great on atmosphere but badly ventilated, chiefly as a result of traditional insulation against the harsh winter.

Musicians entertaining a crowd outside a café in Tallinn.

ESTONIA

FINLAND

0 — 30 — 60 Miles
0 — 50 — 120 Kil

BALTIC SEA

Gulf of Finland

Tallinn Bay
● **TALLINN**

HARJUMAA

Pirita

Rakvere ●
● Kivioli

Kohtla-Järve ●
Sillamäe ●
Narva ●

Kärdla ●

Vormsi Island

Kasari

LÄÄNE - VIRUMAA

Pandivere Plateau

IDA - VIRUMAA

Narva

HIIUMAA

Matsalu State Nature Reserve
● Haapsalu

Rapla ●

Kassäri Island

Matsalu Bay

LÄÄNEMAA

RAPLAMAA

● Paide

JÄRVAMAA

Lake Peipus

Panga Scarp

Muhu Island

Pärnu

Põltsamaa ●

JÕGEVAMAA

SAAREMAA

Karala ●

● Kuressaare

PÄRNUMAA

Pärnu ●

Viljandi ●

VILJANDIMAA

Lake Võrts

Tartu ●
Emajõgi

TARTUMAA

RUSS

Gulf of Riga

Ruhnu Island

Kinhu Island

Otepää Plateau

VÕRUMAA

Vohandu

VALGAMAA

PÕLVAMAA

Valga ●

Haanji Plateau
▲ *Suur Munamägi* (1,040 ft, 317 m)

● Pechory

LATVIA

● Capital city
● Major town
▲ Mountain peak

Feet	Meters
16,500	5,000
9,900	3,000
6,600	2,000
3,300	1,000
1,650	500
660	200
0	0

Baltic Sea, A2

Emajõgi River, D3

Finland, B1
Finland, Gulf of, B2

Haanji Plateau, C4
Haapsalu, B2
Harjumaa, B2
Hiiumaa Island, A2

Ida-Virumaa, D2
Ivangorod, D2

Järvamaa, C3
Jõgevamaa, C3

Karala, A3
Kärdla, A2
Kasari River, B2
Kassari Island, A2
Kinhu Island, B3
Kiviõli, D2
Kohtla-Järve, D2
Kuressaare, A3

Läänemaa, B3
Lääne-Virumaa, C2
Latvia, B4

Matsalu Bay, B3
Matsalu State Nature
    Reserve, B2
Muhu Island, B3

Narva, D2
Narva River, D2

Otepää Plateau, C4

Paide, C3
Pandivere Plateau, C2
Panga Scarp, A3
Pärnu, B3
Pärnu River, B3
Pärnumaa, B3
Pechory, D4
Peipus, Lake, D3
Pirita River, C2
Põltsamaa, C3
Põlvamaa, C4

Rakvere, C2
Rapla, B2
Raplamaa, B3
Riga, Gulf of, B3
Ruhnu Island, A4
Russia, D3

Saaremaa Island, A3
Sillamäe, D2
Suur Munamägi, C4

Tallinn, B2

Tallinn Bay, B2
Tartu, C3
Tartumaa, C3

Valga, C4
Valgamaa, C4
Viljandi, C3
Viljandimaa, C3
Vohandu River, D4
Vormsi Island, B2
Võrts, Lake, C3
Võrumaa, D4

QUICK NOTES

OFFICIAL NAME
Eesti Vabariik (Republic of Estonia)

LAND AREA
17,457 square miles (45,226 square km)

POPULATION
1.5 million (1997 estimate)

CAPITAL
Tallinn

MAJOR CITIES
Tartu, Narva, Kohtla-Järve, Pärnu

COUNTIES (*Maakond*)
Harjumaa, Lääne-Virumaa, Ida-Virumaa, Järvamaa, Jõgevamaa, Viljandimaa, Tartumaa, Põlvamaa, Võrumaa, Valgamaa, Pärnumaa, Läänemaa, Raplamaa, Saaremaa, Hiiumaa

MAJOR RIVERS
Emajõgi, Pärnu, Narva

MAJOR LAKES
Peipus, Võrts

HIGHEST POINT
Suur Manamägi (1,040 feet/317 m)

ETHNIC GROUPS
Estonians (64%), Russians (29%), Ukrainians (2.7%), Belorussians, (1.6%), Finns (1%), and others including Tatars, Jews, Latvians, Poles, Lithuanians, and Germans

RELIGION
Christian—Lutheran, Russian Orthodox, Baptist, Methodist

LANGUAGES
Estonian (official), Latvian, Lithuanian, Russian

CURRENCY
Estonian Kroon (EEK)
US $1 = 12.93 EEK (October 1998)

MAIN EXPORTS
Textiles, timber, wood and paper products, auto parts, mineral products, food, chemicals

MAIN IMPORTS
Machinery, minerals, textiles, chemicals

IMPORTANT ANNIVERSARIES
Independence Day (February 24)—anniversary of the 1918 declaration of independence
Victory Day (June 23)—anniversary of the Battle of Võnnu, 1919

IMPORTANT LEADERS
Lembitu—Estonian tribal leader who resisted the German Knights of the Sword in the 13th century. Killed in Viljandimaa in 1217.
Konstantin Päts (1874–1956)—Radical political leader of Estonia's first period of independence. He ruled Estonia as a "benevolent" dictator in the 1930s.
Lennart Meri (1929–)—Intellectual, historian and writer, he became Estonia's first freely elected president in 1992.

GLOSSARY

Bolsheviks
Russian communists.

glasnost ("GLAHS-nost")
Openness: a policy initiated by Mikhail Gorbachev of the Soviet Union.

head isu ("HEH-uht i-su")
The customary toast before commencing a meal, like "bon appétit."

Jaanipäev ("JAH-ni-pa-ehv")
St. John's Day—An age-old pagan festival of Midsummer celebrated on June 23 and 24.

kannel ("KUHN-ehl")
A musical instrument, like a zither, at least 3,000 years old, with between 5 and 12 iron or natural fiber strings pulled taut over a board. The name derives from a proto-Baltic word meaning "the singing tree."

kissel ("KI-sehl")
A clear, sweet soup made from garden berries and red currants.

kringel ("KRIN-kehl")
A large, braided loaf made from refined white flour. It is prepared in the shape of a pretzel and filled with nuts and raisins. *Kringel* is usually served on birthdays and holidays.

leiva supp ("LEH-iv-uh soop")
A sweet, black bread soup, usually made from leftover bread, eaten as a dessert.

Livonia
Named after the Liv people of Latvia, this region of the Baltic consisting of most of modern Latvia and southern Estonia existed from the 13th century to the early 20th century.

maakond ("MAH-kont")
Counties, of which there are 15 in Estonia.

Maarahvas ("MAH-ruh-vuhs")
"People of the land," the name Estonians give themselves.

pirukas ("PI-ru-kuhs")
Small pies filled with meat, carrots, and cabbage.

Riigikogu ("REE-ki-ko-ku")
The Estonian legislative assembly or parliament.

rosolje ("roh-SOHL-juh")
Salad based on beetroot, potato, meat, and herring, considered typically Estonian.

Rukkileib ("RUK-ki-leh-ip")
Rye bread enhanced with molasses, the favored accompaniment for Estonia's mild cheeses and spicy beer.

Torte ("TORH-teh")
A rich German cake.

Võidupüha ("VO-it-u-pih-hah")
Victory Day, June 23, which is combined with Jaanipäev (see above) to make the Midsummer holiday.

BIBLIOGRAPHY

Cannon, Ilvi Joe and William J.H. Hough. *Guide to Estonia*. Chicago: The Globe Pequot Press, 1995.

Kross, Jaan. *The Czar's Madman*. London: Harper Collins, 1993.

Lieven, Anatol. *The Baltic Revolution: Estonia, Latvia and Lithuania and the Path to Independence*. New Hampshire: Yale University Press, 1993.

Noble, John. *Baltic States and Kaliningrad—A Travel Survival Kit*. Australia: Lonely Planet Publications, 1997.

Pauli, Ulf. *The Baltic States in Facts, Figures and Maps*. London: Janus Publishing Company, 1994.

Thomson, Clare. *The Singing Revolution*. London: Michael Joseph, 1992.

Unwin, Peter. *Baltic Approaches*. London: Michael Russell Ltd, 1996.

Williams, Roger (ed). *Baltic States* (Insight Guides). Hong Kong: APA Publications, 1996.

INDEX

INDEX

INDEX